UNIQUELY OMAHA

101
THINGS
TO KNOW
ABOUT THE
BIG O

MICHAEL KELLY

Omaha World-Herald

TABLE OF CONTENTS

*At left,
Omaha's Old Market*

UNIQUELY OMAHA

By Michael Kelly

Editor Dan Sullivan

Designer Christine Zueck-Watkins

Photo imaging Jolene McHugh

Executive editor Mike Reilly

President and publisher Terry Kroeger

Omaha World-Herald Co., 1314 Douglas St., Omaha, NE 68102-1811

First Edition ISBN: 978-0-692-55512-5

Printed by Walsworth Publishing Co., Marceline, MO

A GOOD PLACE TO LAND

LONG BEFORE I LANDED IN OMAHA, I landed on Omaha. As a kid growing up in Ohio, I played a board game called "Pirate and Traveler" that included a colorful, hard-cover map of the world. I'd spin a dial and move my game piece from city to city, from country to country and across oceans from continent to continent, earning points and collecting cards that told of various locales — all the while watching out for typhoons and pesky pirates.

MICHAEL KELLY

The U.S. part of the world map included 24 cities, one of which I had never heard of — with the exotic name "Omaha." At the age of 8, that was the first I knew of this place in the middle of America. So I was like a lot of people, even today, who had little or no idea about Omaha.

Little did I know that I would spend my adult life living in, learning about and loving Omaha, meanwhile writing about its people, its institutions, its customs, its foibles, its controversies and its recent transformation.

I'm honored that World-Herald editors asked me to tell you about our metropolitan area in "Uniquely Omaha: 101 Things to Know About the Big O."

If you mix together all the elements of this book, the resulting concoction describes one and only one place — Omaha. It's in that sense that this collection of stories, snippets, facts, whimsy and photographs makes us unique. No place else looks exactly like Omaha, a metropolitan area that's cosmopolitan, productive and lively — and yet small enough that neighborhoods actually produce neighbors.

This seems like the perfect time for a book celebrating Omaha. In recent years, the metro area has ranked highly in numerous national socioeconomic and livability lists — so much so that a Chicago newspaper, commenting on a report that an Alpine country was ranked the best place to be born, wryly said in 2015 that "Switzerland is the Omaha of the world." Besides all the cool rankings, our multi-county Omaha metropolitan area is homing in on that million-population milestone, which demographers expect by about 2023. So let's step back, take a breath and appreciate with pride, but also with self-deprecating humor, this place we call home.

You might call Omaha a big small-city or a small big-city. Among U.S. metro areas, Omaha ranks 60th in population. But we are in the top 40 if you count just the folks inside the city limits — about 458,000 in 2015. By either measure — metro or muni — we are far from puny. Our two-state metro area is certainly big compared to surrounding towns and rural communities in America's breadbasket. Then again, it's small next to the nation's megalopolises. Lots of us, though, think Omaha is a right-size city — as Goldilocks might say, not too big and not too small. Just right.

I didn't say perfect. Like any urban area, Omaha is a work in progress — and yet progress is evident. As we work to make it a great place for all who live here, let's take time to celebrate and to explore what makes Omaha ... Omaha.

Maybe you've lived in the Omaha area even longer than my 45 years, or perhaps you're a relative newcomer. Either way, you know there's a lot to enjoy — but in our fast-paced lives, we don't often pause, look around town and appreciate all that we have. Your friends and relatives out of town may be surprised about Omaha, especially if they haven't visited recently or hold misconceptions. (It is not flat. Cows don't wander the streets. Stagecoaches are not our mode of transportation.)

Omaha has changed a lot, especially in the past 20 years or so. A kind of quiet reserve about our city is replaced with steady confidence. We're all for chuckling at ourselves, though, and if outsiders tease us about our city sitting in the middle of nowhere, we're in on the joke. When Bette Midler opened a show at our glittery riverfront arena with a boffo musical number and received a standing ovation, her eyes glistened as she put her hands to her heart and quipped with a sigh of mock sincerity: "Omaha! I've finally made it!" The Omaha audience roared with laughter.

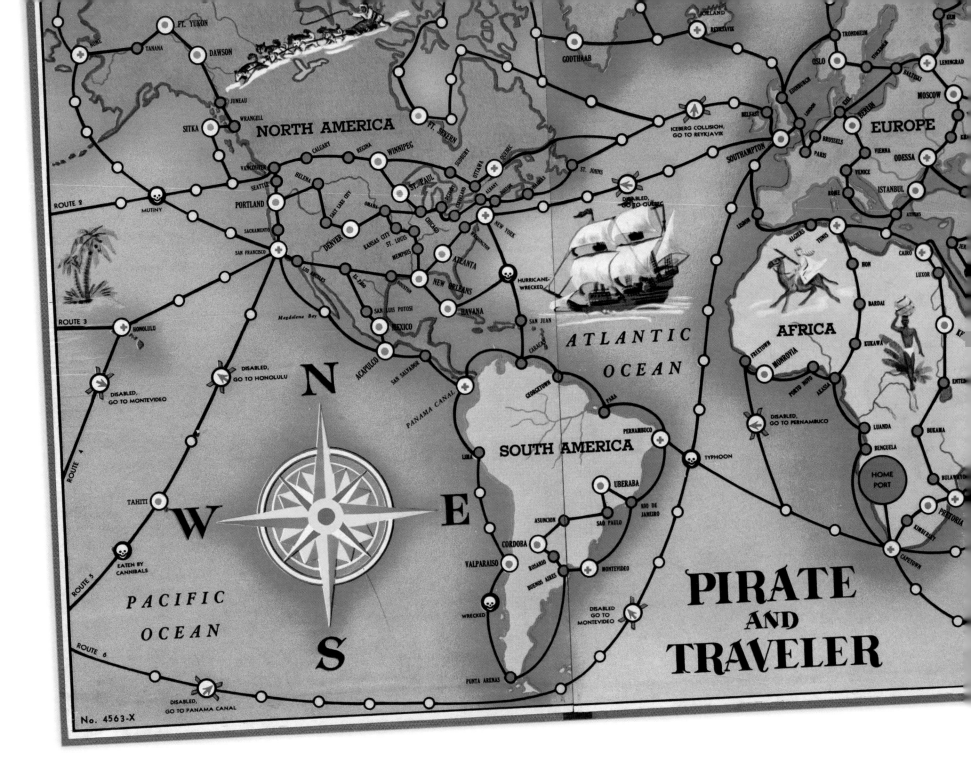

Omaha values straightforward, no-baloney simplicity. Omaha's airport maintains its modest name of Eppley Airfield. The Table Supply Meat Company in the 1960s changed its name to Omaha Steaks. The Mutual Benefit Health & Accident Association became Mutual of Omaha. World-famous investor Warren Buffett, known as the Oracle of Omaha, has maintained a simple lifestyle in spite of his billions, still living in the modest house he bought near Memorial Park and Elmwood Park in 1958.

So let's take a straightforward look at what connects us, and at what it's like living together at this time in this place among these people. We Omahans hold our own strong opinions and surely don't agree on everything, and we may have differing backgrounds. But we live on the same turf close to the same river and under the same skies. In many ways, we're more alike than we are different.

For me, Omaha was a good place to have landed — *on* Omaha in a board game as a kid; and *in* Omaha to work and raise a family as an adult. Lucky me. Let's collect some thoughts and connect some dots about 21st century folks who share this time and space. A place in the middle of America called Omaha.

"A few enterprising pioneers get together and arrive at the conclusion that right here ... is to rise a mighty city."

— Omaha businessman Daniel W. Carpenter, describing the early days of frontier towns

THE BASICS

Let's get started with a primer on Omaha. Even though it still sits
in the middle of the country, it's become a far different place —
vibrant, lively, optimistic and proud. People from elsewhere are starting
to notice. Hey, we didn't make up all those high national rankings.

1. A VIBRANT STORY

1803 Nebraska Territory was part of the Louisiana Purchase, and the next year Meriwether Lewis and William Clark embarked with their Corps of Discovery. Along the way, they decamped on the banks of the Missouri at what became Omaha. Just south of today's Eppley Airfield, according to Clark's journal, they fought off mosquitoes. Fur traders later set up shop just south, in present-day Bellevue.

1846 Mormons led by Brigham Young set up Winter Quarters in today's Florence area of Omaha during their trek to Salt Lake City. A beautiful Mormon temple sits on a hilltop next to the cemetery where some who died that awful winter are buried. A statue of Young stands amid them.

1854 "Omaha City" was founded alongside America's longest river, the 2,341-mile-long Muddy Mo. A few years later, Abraham Lincoln, before he was president, stood on a promontory just east of the river in Iowa and looked across toward fledgling Omaha. In 1863, President Lincoln declared that Council Bluffs and Omaha would be the eastern terminus of the transcontinental railroad. Just as President John F. Kennedy in the early 1960s had set a goal of landing men on the moon before the '60s decade was out, the railroad linking East and West also was completed before a '60s decade ended: the railroad, 1869; the moon landing, 1969.

1860s When the Union Pacific started laying rails westward, there was no bridge over the Missouri. So work began at Seventh and Chicago Streets, site of today's CenturyLink Center, Omaha's gleaming convention center and arena. In a sense, the U.P. built Omaha, and its national headquarters today stands in a glass-encased building downtown.

LATE 1800s The South Omaha Stockyards became a big, smelly and bloody business, though the odor that emanated from the area was called "the smell of money." The kill floors provided many jobs that attracted immigrants to the slaughterhouses, which became known by the euphemistic term "meatpacking plants." Descendants of those hardworking immigrants include many in the city's educated, professional class.

In the first third of the 20th century, Omaha was ruled unofficially but powerfully by "Boss" Tom Dennison. Reformers finally prevailed in the 1930s, and Omaha later adopted a new city charter and a strong-mayor form of government that still exists. The mayor is the full-time chief executive of the City of Omaha, with a City Council member elected in each of seven districts.

AFTER **WWII** The postwar era in Omaha, as elsewhere, brought great growth and an expansion of schools to accommodate the baby-boom generation. The nation's first indoor shopping center, The Center, opened at 42nd and Center Streets in 1955, though downtown with its department stores, such as Brandeis, remained the primary shopping area. But things were changing. The Crossroads Mall opened at 72nd and Dodge Streets in 1960, and more people began moving to new subdivisions on the city's southwest side. That was fueled in part by construction of Interstate 80, which opened in 1962 and headed southwest toward the state capital of Lincoln and beyond.

1960S Omaha's skyline was changing. At times over the objections of preservationists, many historical buildings were demolished. They included the U.S. Post Office, the City Hall, the Fontenelle Hotel and the old Woodmen of the World Building, as well as, in the '80s, 19th-century warehouses east of 10th Street and near the river, an area known as Jobbers Canyon. City officials said it would have cost too much to renovate those old buildings.

Downtown declined as a shopping area, and department stores **1970S** sprang up in malls with lots of free parking. Mayor Gene Leahy, in office from 1969 to 1973, espoused a "return to the river" movement downtown, urging redevelopment of Omaha's drab and dirty riverfront. An early step was to clear out four linear blocks of old downtown buildings in the 1970s, creating a lagoon and the Central Park Mall, later renamed the Leahy Mall. Around the same time, the old fruit and vegetable wholesale market centered at 11th and Howard Streets began emerging as an Omaha attraction known for its brick streets, carriage rides, restaurants and quaint shops — still today a popular gathering point for tourists and locals alike, known as the Old Market.

In the past two decades, Omaha has completed its transfor- **21ST** CENTURY mation. Evidence abounds, including high national rankings in a raft of economic studies and surveys. Besides that, the physical appearance has greatly improved, starting with the city's front porch: The formerly drab and dirty riverfront, long home to a polluting lead-smelting plant, a junkyard and a railroad-repair yard, now features a convention center and arena, a new baseball stadium, a gathering place for concerts and festivals, and walking and biking trails.

2. A DISTINCTIVE NAME

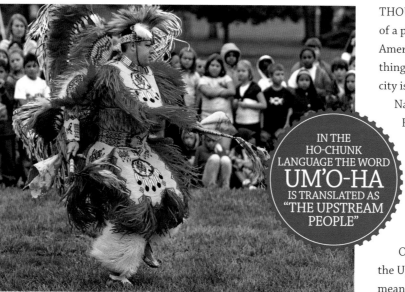

IN THE HO-CHUNK LANGUAGE THE WORD **UM'O-HA** IS TRANSLATED AS "THE UPSTREAM PEOPLE"

THOUGH MOST WIDELY KNOWN as the name of a place nearly smack dab in the middle of America, the word "Omaha" means different things to different people. Nebraska's largest city is named for the Omaha Indian tribe.

Native Americans moved west from the Ohio River Valley, one group heading south and the other going upstream on the Missouri River. Today, the Omaha Tribe is based on a mostly impoverished reservation in Macy, Nebraska, about 70 miles north of the mostly prosperous city of Omaha.

A restaurant in an old firehouse in Omaha's popular Old Market area is called the Upstream, the name inspired by the Indian meaning for Omaha.

3. NAMESAKES

A MOMENT IN HISTORY

"Omaha Beach" was the code name for an American landing area on D-Day, June 6, 1944, where casualties were so heavy that it is known to history as "Bloody Omaha." The reason the area was named for Omaha never has been conclusively explained, but a 2008 World-Herald article reported an intriguing tale. The family of the late Gayle Eyler, a carpenter on the staff of Gen. Omar Bradley in World War II and later the chief housing inspector for the City of Omaha, found a note that Eyler had written. Though he had never spoken to his family about it, the note said that Bradley had chosen the name Omaha in appreciation for his carpenter. Military officials said code names often were selected at random and that the explanation couldn't be dismissed.

ETC.

Omaha is also the name of four other U.S. towns, in Arkansas, Georgia, Illinois and Texas, and is the name of a tony place in New Zealand.

FIRST TO THE FINISH LINE

Omaha was the name of the 1935 Thoroughbred that won the Triple Crown of racing, one of only 12 horses to win the Kentucky Derby, the Preakness Stakes and the Belmont Stakes.

THE NEW BLACK

Omaha also is a color – Omaha Orange. It is used across the country on highway cones and barrels and also is known as safety orange. Allied Van Lines, which paints its trucks in that hue, says it inherited the color from its 1928 originator, the Ford Storage and Moving Company of Omaha. "Our founder, Mr. Ford ... came from a rather thrifty generation and was therefore looking for a good deal on paint," Allied says. "When the painter offered him a very reasonable price for all his 'leftovers,' Mr. Ford quickly agreed. The resulting mixture became Omaha Orange."

A WINNING HAND

It's a poker game called Omaha Hold 'Em, combining community cards that are visible with cards hidden in bettors' hands.

THE NAME "OMAHA" HAS LOTS OF OTHER MEANINGS

THE ROAD TO OMAHA

THE ULTIMATE DESTINATION

For college baseball players, Omaha is not only a geographic location but a symbol, a holy grail. As home of the College World Series since 1950, the word "Omaha" is spoken almost reverently by players and coaches as the ultimate destination. In the locker room at Louisiana State University, a school that frequently has made it to the CWS, players daily see a sign with one word in letters 3 feet high: OMAHA. Retired NCAA official Dennis Poppe said ballplayers don't say they hope to make it to the national championship series. "They say they want to go to Omaha."

A SECRET SIGNAL

In 2014, Peyton Manning of the Denver Broncos caused a sensation during the NFL playoffs by repeatedly calling out "Omaha!" at the line of scrimmage. It was either code to his teammates or it meant nothing at all. But tourism directors across the U.S. expressed envy that the city of Omaha got a little free publicity. Omaha businesses, meanwhile, pledged donations to Manning's charity for at-risk kids for every time he called the city's name. He later came to Omaha to accept a check for about $70,000.

4. SPIRIT OF REVIVAL

THE CITY IN THE MIDDLE of the country finds itself in the midst of a renaissance. Have people in the rest of the country noticed? Not necessarily. Surveys have shown that Omaha doesn't have a bad image — it just doesn't have much of an image. What has changed, though, is how Omahans feel about where they live. There's a new self-image.

If we previously bordered on an inferiority complex, well, today there's a proud, quiet confidence. Nationally known writer and public-radio host Kurt Andersen, an Omaha native, wrote in the New York Times that he once had given up on his hometown. But the tide turned, he said, and Omaha had undergone a "cultural awakening."

To appreciate how much things have changed, look back to Omaha's nadir, the late 1980s. Much of the news was negative, including the loss of 2,000 good jobs when a prominent company, Enron, was moved out of town. ConAgra, a Fortune 500 company, also threatened to leave.

So what happened? The corporate community got behind a legislative package of tax incentives, and ConAgra stayed to build an extensive campus near the riverfront.

First National Bank considered building 10 miles west of downtown but decided in the late '90s to build a 45-story downtown office tower. Some call that another turning point.

A national consultant's study, meanwhile, recommended that Omaha's good reputation as a hard-working town and a fine place to raise families needed an injection of something else — fun and "sparkle." After decades of studies about whether to replace the 1954 Omaha Civic Auditorium, an aging center for sports, entertainment and trade shows, voters in 2000 overwhelmingly approved a $216 million bond issue to build a convention center and arena — yet another milestone in Omaha's transformation.

Omaha's formerly drab and dirty riverfront benefited from addition by subtraction with the removal of a web of railroad tracks winding past decades-old industrial plants.

DOWNTOWN OMAHA: THEN AND NOW

"The riverfront remake of late is part of Omaha's new confidence," said a 2014 travel article, "but there is something else: A refocus and rediscovery is taking place in some of Omaha's downtown and close-in neighborhoods."

5. RANKINGS

OMAHA WON'T COAST, AND IT NEEDN'T BOAST. BUT IT'S NICE IF OTHERS BRAG ON US.

"The great thing about Omaha is the public-private partnerships to keep the downtown revitalized, to keep the kids well-educated, to make it a fun, vibrant city. You know, I went to Omaha. I came away blown away by the vision and the fun that you can have in Nebraska."

Robert Frick of Kiplinger's, who extolled the city on CNBC, noting a "ridiculous (low) unemployment rate."

MODEST AS WE ARE in Omaha, we have to just shake our heads and smile in amazement at the numerous national rankings. They are nice for us to know, but is anyone else noticing how often the Big O sits at or near the top of many "best of" lists? We wondered. But then it happened. In 2015, a Chicago Sun-Times editorial startlingly said: "Switzerland is the Omaha of the world."

The newspaper was commenting on an international livability survey that named the alpine country the best nation in which to be born. And as an analogy, the editorial cited Omaha — not specifically saying it was the best birthplace, but noting that it regularly ranks high in livability surveys.

No, Omaha doesn't have Alps. But if you like rankings, a mountain of evidence points to our town being a really good place to live. As with any urban area, Omaha still is working to get better and solve problems so that everyone can enjoy living here. But the list of high rankings is so long that it's clear we have a lot going for us. Critics may dismiss the notion that, like the Swiss, we Omahans are big cheeses of livability. But outsiders, not Omahans, created these rankings:

1ST
BEST CITY TO RAISE A FAMILY IN AMERICA — Movoto real estate blog, January 2014
UNO IS BEST COLLEGE FOR VETERANS FOR 2015 — Military Times, December 2014

2ND
BEST CITIES TO GET A JOB IN — Business.com, September 2015
CITIES WITH HIGH SALARIES AND LOW COSTS OF LIVING — GoBankingRates.com, September 2014
BEST CITIES FOR PROFESSIONAL WOMEN — Movoto blog, March 2014
LEAST CONGESTED BIG CITIES — HomeInsurance.com, June 2014
TOP CITIES FOR RETIRING BABY BOOMERS — (Omaha-Council Bluffs), Builder, December 2014
BEST CITIES TO GROW OLDER IN — CNN Money, November 2014
BEST CITIES TO START A SMALL BUSINESS — UpCounsel, May 2015

3RD
MOST AFFORDABLE BIG CITIES IN THE U.S. — Kiplinger, October 2014
BEST CITIES TO LAUNCH A STARTUP — CNN Money, October 2014
HARDEST-WORKING TOWNS IN AMERICA — the SpareFoot Blog, August 2014
BEST CITIES FOR YOUNG PROFESSIONALS — Forbes, August 2014

4TH
BEST CITIES TO FLIP A HOUSE — (Omaha-Council Bluffs), 24/7 Wall St., May 2014
AMERICA'S BEST CITIES FOR RAISING A FAMILY — Forbes, April 2014

5TH
BEST METRO AREAS FOR STEM PROFESSIONALS — (Omaha-Council Bluffs), Wallethub.com, January 2015
BEST CITIES FOR QUALITY OF LIFE — Nerdwallet.com, August 2014
TOP METROS FOR GREEN-FRIENDLY APARTMENTS — Apartment Guide, February 2014

6TH
GREAT AFFORDABLE COLLEGE TOWNS IN THE U.S. — Great Value Colleges, August 2014
BEST CITIES FOR STAYCATIONS — Wallethub.com, June 2014

7TH
BEST CITIES TO FIND A JOB — Wallethub.com, January 2015
BEST CITIES FOR JOB SEEKERS — Nerdwallet.com, January 2014
MOST AFFORDABLE BIG CITIES IN THE U.S. — the Simple Dollar, July 2014

8TH
BEST CITIES FOR CONSUMER BANKING — Nerdwallet.com, January 2014

9TH
TOP FOODIE CITIES — Livability, 2014

10TH
BEST CITIES FOR YOUNG ENTREPRENEURS — Nerdwallet.com, November 2014
TOP CITIES FOR YOUNG ENTREPRENEURS — Forbes, November 2014

6. THE BUZZ

OMAHA IS FAR FROM PERFECT, but we have to chuckle at disparaging comments from others who look down their noses — out their airplane windows, presumably — at us sad sacks who live down in Flyover Country. At the same time, many have sung Omaha's praises. With a smile, or an occasional wince at a barb, enjoy a helping or two of comments about our town in recent years:

 **LISTEN TO THESE GUYS**

The Wall Street Journal called Omaha *"one of the nation's biggest success stories."*

- - - - - - - - - - - - - - - - - - -

Kiplinger's Personal Finance noted Omaha's quality of jobs and its *"stereo-type-busting cultural scene."*

"Instead of falling backward economically as so many other cities have in recent years," said Delta Airlines' Sky magazine, *"Omaha has been too busy moving forward, accomplishing the things that most cities can only dare to dream."*

A Kansas City Star columnist wrote that K.C. officials should get on a bus and look at the city to the north, saying, *"Afterward, I'd fire anyone who fails to be excited about the possibilities for Kansas City after seeing what Omaha has accomplished in the last few years."*

A writer for the London Independent wrote of Omaha's *"vast new convention center"* and *"a number of other striking new buildings in the downtown area. Omaha itself has become a very prosperous place, which now stretches out, seemingly interminably, into the Midwest plains."*

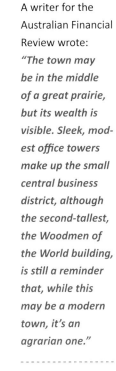

USA Today wrote that Omaha, *"about as far away from both Wall Street and Silicon Valley as you can get,"* had blossomed from a town of meatpackers into a major hub of business. The article added that Omaha has *"tremendous wealth, industry and influence for being in the middle of nowhere."*

A writer for the Australian Financial Review wrote: *"The town may be in the middle of a great prairie, but its wealth is visible. Sleek, modest office towers make up the small central business district, although the second-tallest, the Woodmen of the World building, is still a reminder that, while this may be a modern town, it's an agrarian one."*

- - - - - - - - - - - - - - - - - -

A Dallas Morning News article headlined "Dusting Off Omaha's Image" said: *"Within the last few years, the city has transformed the riverfront from an industrial wasteland into a modern, manicured and walkable extension of downtown, where there's a hip makeover making waves."*

The Colorado Springs Gazette called Omaha *"one of the more successful cities over the last 25 years"* and said it had *"garnered national recognition for its resurgent downtown."*

- - - - - - - - - - - - - - - - - -

A Washington, D.C., correspondent for the American Spectator wrote: *"When I visited Omaha, Nebraska, I became a much friendlier version of myself."*

- - - - - - - - - - - - - - - - - -

The Los Angeles-based Milken Institute, a nonpartisan think tank, said the Omaha-Council Bluffs metro area had *"zoomed up in the rankings of best-performing U.S. cities."*

The great thing about Omaha Steaks, a male WNYW reporter in New York said, is that you can have the steaks sent without ever having to go to Omaha. A female anchor interrupted, saying, *"I have actually heard that Omaha is a very cool town, one of the coolest towns in central Nebraska."*

- - - - - - - - - - - - - - - - - -

A San Diego columnist who had visited years earlier, wrote: *"I have never had any reason to go (back) to Omaha, but even if I were compelled to do so, I would summon up an excuse never to set foot in Omaha."*

- - - - - - - - - - - - - - - - - -

A New York Post writer referred to *"sleepy Omaha, Nebraska,"* known as *"a cow-and-corn town"* and *"a yawner city."*

- - - - - - - - - - - - - - - - - -

A New Yorker magazine critic said director Alexander Payne's work had featured *"the dead-eyed blandness of Omaha"* and *"the emotional flatness and evasiveness of the place."*

The Sunday Times of London wrote that for most of the year — except for the weekend of the Berkshire Hathaway shareholder meeting — Omaha is a *"mediocre little town in Nebraska of no interest to the rest of the world."*

- - - - - - - - - - - - - - - - - -

In U.K. publications, an outraged British professor was upset at a TV plot twist that included a "shameful" historical inaccuracy. *"The series was made,"* he fumed, *"with the original intention of dumbing it down so that even an audience in Omaha, Nebraska, could understand it."*

- - - - - - - - - - - - - - - - - -

A San Francisco Chronicle article about plastic surgery and $7,000 nose jobs looked down its nose at Omaha. *"There's certainly an attitude of California to look your best,"* a surgeon said. *"You can tell the difference between standing at the corner in Los Angeles and standing at the corner in Omaha."*

7. WEATHERING OUR SEASONS

OMAHA'S HOTTEST MONTH

JULY 1936

Really, it was so hot on July 4, 1936, that you could fry an egg on the pavement. The daily high averaged 100.4 during the month, with an all-time high, 114 degrees, on July 25.

OMAHA'S COLDEST MONTH

DECEMBER 1983

The temperature didn't climb above zero for a record 203 consecutive hours, more than eight days. The temperature dropped as low as 24 below zero on one of the nights, and the high on one day was minus 11. (Omaha's all-time low of 32 below zero occurred January 5, 1885.)

OMAHA IS A REALLY cool town. Lots going on, lots to do, lots of cool, creative folks. Really cool. And, uh, at times *really* cool. The Weather Channel, in fact, ranks Omaha as the fifth-coldest major city in the United States. We're in good company, though, with Minneapolis-St. Paul first, then Anchorage, Alaska; Madison, Wisconsin; Milwaukee; and, right behind us, Chicago. Hardy cities all, and hardly any reason to feel sorry for them.

Don't feel sorry for Omaha, either. After all, it's not always cold here. Take summer, for example, which occasionally gets ungodly hot and humid. Yes, our weather can get a little extreme, which doesn't mean Omaha isn't an extremely fine place to live. It's just that we occasionally have to, well, weather our environs.

But unless you live in San Diego, who doesn't? The problem is our extremes. Omaha sits in the middle of the country, a "continental" climate far from the seas, which causes intemperate summer and winter variations. So, no, we don't brag about our weather. But we do brag about The Change of Seasons. (The joke is that seasonal change can occur daily.) We love the promise of spring, the beauty of autumn, the bracing cold of winter, the shirtsleeves of summer. Variety is life's spice, and we take pleasure in contemplating Earth's beauty. San Diego can keep its boring weather.

THE AVERAGE YEAR-ROUND TEMPERATURE IS ABOUT 52, WHICH ALSO HAPPENS TO BE THE NATIONAL AVERAGE.

ARGUING THAT OUR WEATHER IS GREAT WOULD BE LIKE SAYING THAT IF YOU PUT YOUR HEAD IN THE FREEZER AND YOUR FEET IN THE OVEN, ON AVERAGE YOU'RE COMFORTABLE.

EXTREMES

MAY 2013

You like variety? Omaha went from a daily record low of 32 degrees on May 12, 2013, to a daily record high of 101 two days later. May 14 became the earliest in the year that Omaha had reached triple digits. That month also was the city's snowiest May on record, with 3.1 inches on May 1 and 2.

STORMS

We never see a hurricane, let alone a tsunami, and are at little risk for earthquakes, though we have to keep an eye out for tornadoes. Omaha's Class AAA professional baseball team, a longtime affiliate of the Kansas City Royals, after all, is called the Storm Chasers.

ATTRACTIONS

Visitors are coming, so how to give them a feel for what makes Omaha real? Lots of attractions beckon. Your cousins or business associates surely would enjoy our acclaimed zoo, the botanical gardens, the riverfront, Boys Town and the Old Market, along with other biggies in the Big O.

8. *HENRY DOORLY ZOO & AQUARIUM*

OMAHA'S HENRY DOORLY ZOO & AQUARIUM is home to North America's largest cat complex, the world's largest glazed geodesic dome and indoor desert, the world's largest nocturnal exhibit, the second-largest free-flight aviary and one of the world's largest indoor rainforests. Director Dennis Pate (below) is overseeing a master plan of improvements that include an African Grasslands exhibit unveiled in 2015. Besides all that visitors see, the Omaha zoo is known for its scientific research in trying to save the world's tigers, lemurs, coral reefs and endangered plants, as well as for breeding cheetahs and for its other behind-the-scenes activities in the Center for Conservation and Research. The zoo is a leader in reproductive research and produced the world's first test-tube and artificially inseminated tigers. Its work in foreign countries has been lauded by National Geographic. But families that ride the overhead Skyfari and the zoo train, view the penguins and the sharks in the aquarium or watch films at the IMAX theater come not just for education but also for a day of great fun.

HOW IT BEGAN

Omaha's expansive 155-acre zoo sits on a bluff high above the Missouri River in the former Riverview Park, which was founded in 1894. The zoo's eventual namesake, Henry Doorly (below), joined the Omaha World-Herald as a reporter in 1903 and retired as board chairman in 1960. In 1963, his widow, Margaret "Peggy" Doorly, called the Omaha zoo pathetic. She donated $750,000, the equivalent of more than $5 million in 2015, and the zoo was named for her late husband. Its official reopening was April 1, 1967.

WORLD'S
BEST ZOO
HENRY DOORLY
ZOO & AQUARIUM
— TripAdvisor,
2014

In February 1971, an Indian rhinoceros named Tiny had to be tranquilized and taken to Iowa State University veterinary hospital for surgery to remove an intestinal obstruction. Dr. Lee Simmons guided him into a heated truck.

IT'S A JUNGLE OUT THERE

A zoo isn't just a place with cuddly animals. Injuries and death occur. In 1976, five Sumatran tigers died from lung problems. In 1987, a male tiger killed a female. In 1992, three stray dogs yapped at high-strung wallabies, which ran wildly into fences — 25 of them died of injury or fright. In 2001, a gibbon killed and consumed an exotic bird in front of 100 people at the Lied Jungle. At a zoo, life happens. The zoo has it own hospital, but in rare cases animals are treated elsewhere. In 2012, a 432-pound gorilla named Motuba, or "Tubby," fractured his upper jaw in a fall when pushed by another gorilla. Zoo vets arranged to take Tubby, unannounced on a Saturday morning, to the Nebraska Medical Center, where he had surgery. The story was told around the country and overseas.

NO TRUTH TO THE RUMOR

Several years back, a crazy story about a child taking a penguin home from the zoo reached the status of urban legend. Dr. Lee Simmons says he would occasionally receive calls asking about a boy who talked in the family car on the way home about "a new friend" and the parents' shock to discover a small penguin in a backpack. "If you ever smelled one..." the former zoo director said. "Well, it would be hard for anyone to smuggle it home."

"Hang onto your hat, because it's only going to get better."

— Director Dennis Pate, on carrying out the vision set by Lee Simmons

DIRECTOR **DENNIS PATE** IS THE NATIONAL CHAIRMAN OF THE ASSOCIATION OF ZOOS AND AQUARIUMS

ZOO FUNDING

THE ZOO'S ECONOMIC IMPACT IS NEARLY **$100 MILLION** A YEAR

The City of Omaha provides the zoo no direct tax money, but it receives more than $1 million a year from keno gambling. Donations, membership fees and admissions keep it financially healthy.

Near Ashland, Nebraska, the zoo also operates the 40-acre Simmons Safari Park, a drive-through experience.

HIGH SCORES

FamilyFun magazine named Omaha's zoo the No. 1 animal attraction, ahead of those in St. Louis, San Diego and Cincinnati, and Disney's Animal Kingdom in Orlando.

Touropia.com in 2013 ranked Omaha's zoo No. 1 in size ahead of those in Moscow, Beijing and the Bronx, saying: "Although there are bigger zoos in terms of acreage or species numbers, none rank as high if both of these categories are combined."

LEE "DOC" SIMMONS

Simmons arrived in 1966 and became zoo director in 1970. No one could foresee what would unfold, not even Doc himself. But he kept coming up with ideas, and Omaha donors kept coming up with money.

The public increasingly bought memberships in droves (the most per-capita in the country), and the zoo staff under Simmons increased from 10 to nearly 300.

When he became zoo director, total attendance was 280,000. That grew to 470,000 in 1983 and to 1 million by 1992. Attendance reached a record of 1.7 million in 2012. "His visions became our visions," former assistant zoo director Randy Wisthoff once said. "He's a guy on a mission, and we're happy to be along."

A lot has happened over the years at The House That Doc Built. Friends enjoyed teasing Simmons about always wearing brown on the job, but beneath his plain-brown-wrapper exterior lies a mind that has raced with ideas.

Besides his vision, Simmons for nearly a half-century has maintained a good relationship with the public, donors and board members. Said Wisthoff: "It's just a perfect marriage between Lee and people in this community."

Simmons is president of the zoo's foundation.

UNDER LEE SIMMONS, ANNUAL ATTENDANCE GREW FROM 280,000 TO **1.7 MILLION**

ZOO BABIES

Babies of almost any species are popular at the zoo, but their tenure isn't long-lasting. Most youngsters stay only a couple of years, depending on the species, before heading off to other zoos, where they will play a role in further breeding efforts.

AQUARIUM

The Suzanne and Walter Scott Aquarium displays aquatic habitats from the poles, temperate oceans, coral reefs and the Amazon. Visitors also can view birds, including dozens of penguins.

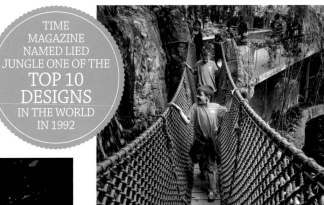

TIME MAGAZINE NAMED LIED JUNGLE ONE OF THE **TOP 10 DESIGNS** IN THE WORLD IN 1992

AFRICAN GRASSLANDS

Giraffes moved into their new digs at the zoo's African Grasslands in 2015.

THE DESERT DOME STANDS **13 STORIES TALL**

DESERT DOME

The dome covers exhibits from three deserts: the Southwest U.S., Australia and southern Africa.

9. *THE OLD MARKET*

THE OLD MARKET, dating to the turn of the 20th century and earlier, is a local attraction, not just a tourist mecca. The old fruit and vegetable market, 24 blocks of mostly brick streets downtown, is Omaha Cool. With horse-drawn carriages, street performers, upscale and midscale restaurants, art and photo galleries, salons, gift, antique and coffee shops, clothing and furniture stores, boutiques, taverns, live music, apartments, condos and even a couple of hotels, the Old Market seems old in name only. It is all about what's good in the new Omaha.

The focal point is the intersection of 11th and Howard Streets, where one can look in all directions and see converted warehouses put to lively, modern uses. People walk along covered sidewalks, with flowers planted above. Young and old stroll around or just sit and engage in people-watching.

"WILL BECOME AN ICON IN URBAN AMERICA"
— City planner from Columbus, OH

"THE NEW ORLEANS OF THE NORTH"
— Minnesota travel writer

MARK MERCER

Mark Mercer (above), son of Old Market founder Sam Mercer (below right), has a tumble of white hair like his late father's —and no plans to alter his dad's vision of the area as a vibrant shopping mecca of independent, local businesses. Always looking for new ideas, Mark for more than 20 years has run Mercer Management, the area's main property owner. But he also has fostered relationships with other landlords and says they agree on retaining the tone and look of the Old Market.

The first Mercers came to Omaha in 1866, and the family ended up owning many downtown buildings. Sam Mercer was the central force behind the 1960s redevelopment of warehouses in the old fruit and vegetable market, with restaurants, shops and lofts along brick streets. Mark has carried on and preserved the legacy of his father, who saved old buildings when some called for a wrecking ball.

OLD MARKET MAINSTAYS

Many of the shops, restaurants and bars have stayed for decades. Some of the places that have made the Old Market a beloved Omaha locale:

- Mr. Toad's
- V. Mertz
- M's Pub
- Billy Frogg's
- La Buvette
- Nouvelle Eve
- Ted & Wally's
- Tannenbaum
- Upstream
- Souq
- Omaha Prime
- Passageway Gallery
- Spaghetti Works

"No Sam Mercer, no Old Market."

— Marty Shukert, a former City of Omaha planning director

10. JOSLYN ART MUSEUM

THE JOSLYN MUSEUM FEATURES OVER **11,000** WORKS FROM ANTIQUE TO PRESENT

A Dale Chihuly glass sculpture, weighing 15,000 pounds and with more than 2,080 pieces, was a 2000 gift from Walter and Suzanne Scott. Their names grace the Scott Pavilion, a 58,000-square-foot addition to the museum in 1994.

"The money was made in Omaha, and it will be spent here."

— Sarah Joslyn, who donated more than $8 million for the project

OMAHANS TODAY ENJOY many amenities that resulted in large part from donations. The wealthy have contributed amply toward modern projects such as the CenturyLink Center convention center and arena, TD Ameritrade Park and the Holland Performing Arts Center. Donors of the 21st century follow the great example of an early-20th century Omahan, Sarah Joslyn.

The Joslyn Art Museum, with its Georgia pink-marble exterior, is an Art Deco masterpiece. It opened in 1931 in memory of her late husband, businessman George Joslyn, who had struck it rich in the late 19th century with "ready print" inside pages for small newspapers.

The museum today holds a comprehensive permanent collection. It includes Titian, Renoir, Degas, Monet and Rembrandt as well as more than 400 drawings by Swiss artist Karl Bodmer, based on his 1832-34 journey to the Missouri River frontier. The extensive museum collection ranges from Greek pottery to abstract pieces by Jackson Pollock. Temporary exhibits rotate in and out each year. A beautiful fountain court sits just east of the museum's Witherspoon Concert Hall. In 2013, the museum stopped charging general admission, providing free access as it had until the mid-1960s.

The Joslyn "surveys the fields of Nebraska from a pristine 1931 Art Deco structure, combining Renoir and Monet with Native American painting and sculpture."

— The London Independent, which gave the Joslyn "artistic exclamation marks"

JOSLYN CASTLE

A mile to the west of the Joslyn Art Museum sits the Joslyn Castle, where Sarah Joslyn's ghost is said to walk at night. Well, it was built in 1903, so maybe the four-story, 34-room Scottish Baronial mansion just creaks a bit. In any case, it is well cared for. The Castle, which the Joslyns called Lynhurst, is an Omaha architectural treasure. Sarah lived on the 5.5-acre estate until she died in 1940 at 88. From 1944 to 1989, it served as headquarters for the Omaha Public Schools. To preserve the structure, the State of Nebraska took ownership in the 1990s, and the nonprofit Joslyn Castle Trust bought it in 2010. The 19,360-square-foot Castle includes a reception hall, music room, ballroom, library and drawing room, with a formal entrance and an ornate staircase. Its beauty includes carved wood, stained glass, chiseled stone, mosaic tiles and wrought iron. The building is open for events and public visits.

11. DURHAM MUSEUM

THE OLD UNION STATION was a train depot for 40 years and now has served as a museum for 40 years. But the five years in between those two stretches were the problem. The building was closed and dilapidated, and it suffered water and pigeon damage. Many feared that it would be razed.

The Union Pacific had given it to the City of Omaha, but critics called it a white elephant, too costly to save. Basic repairs were made, though, and a small cadre of railroad enthusiasts opened a "Western Heritage" museum on a shoestring in 1975, with little more than a model railroad, a slide display and a gun collection. A World-Herald headline said: "'Poor Boy' Museum Chugs Along." In the years since, lots of folks contributed ideas, hard work and money — about $30 million in capital improvements, much of it starting in the 1990s — and today it's a Smithsonian-affiliated museum.

The stunningly renovated concourse is home to the annual Christmas at Union Station and other events. Named for donors Charles W. and Margre Durham, the museum just south of downtown and the Old Market is one of Omaha's gems. The wrecking ball, fortunately, never arrived. And a 2015 exhibit was titled: "Union Station: Built to Last."

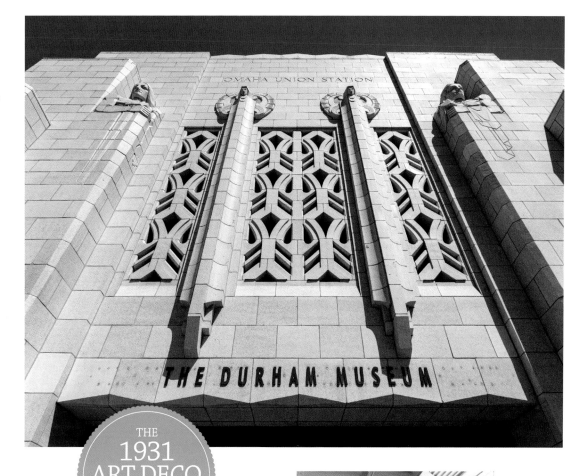

THE
1931
ART DECO
BUILDING HAS A
TERRA COTTA
EXTERIOR

ON THE OLD TRACK LEVEL

- Climb aboard restored passenger-train cars and an old streetcar.
- Tour a museum of Omaha history.
- Visit an auditorium and see national traveling exhibits.
- Walk through a replica of the old Buffett Grocery, where young Warren Buffett worked for his uncle.

12. BOB KERREY PEDESTRIAN BRIDGE

IT USED TO BE EASY to ignore an important fact about the Omaha metropolitan area — a river runs through it. And not just any river. It's the Missouri, the Muddy Mo, the longest river in the United States. But until the removal of a century-old riverfront smelting plant and other eyesores in recent years, access to the banks was difficult. Now people not only can get close to the river but can get right on top of it — or just above it — on the spectacular Bob Kerrey Pedestrian Bridge. The S-shaped span, its twin pylons rising 200 feet and lighted at night, stretches 3,000 feet, including the landings. The "cable-stay" structure was dedicated in 2008 and named for the Medal of Honor recipient who lost part of a leg in Vietnam and became a Nebraska governor and U.S. senator. The 15-foot-wide walkway, as high as 60 feet above the water, has attracted walkers and bicyclists and connects trails on the two sides. And, hey, if you've ever wanted to be in two places at once, well, you can do it in the middle of the bridge — straddling the line that marks the boundary between Iowa and Nebraska.

THE BOB KERREY
BRIDGE IS THE
LONGEST
PEDESTRIAN BRIDGE
LINKING
TWO STATES

OMAHA IS A CROSSROADS

Omaha sits at the point where the nation's longest river crosses the nation's second-longest Interstate highway, I-80. (I-90 is longer.) But the river has flowed for thousands of years, long before any highways. Lewis and Clark's Corps of Discovery traveled up the Missouri starting in 1804 and camped near today's Eppley Airfield. At today's Lewis and Clark National Historic Trail Visitor Center next to the Kerrey bridge, the National Park Service commemorates the expedition that opened the American West.

13. THE GENE LEAHY MALL

OMAHA IS HOME to a beautiful mall that has no stores, food courts or escalators — the Gene Leahy Mall. It's a mall not in the latter-day sense of a shopping center but rather in the traditional meaning of "a shaded walk or promenade," like the National Mall in Washington, D.C. The Leahy Mall has made a significant impact on the resurgence of downtown Omaha.

With a lagoon running through it, the six-block-long parkland sits well below street level and features waterfalls, public art, a wood-plank footbridge, pathways, two big slides and a grassy, sloping landscape. Its eastern edge sits near the lake at Heartland of America Park. Omaha's main public library sits at the western edge, the dazzling Holland Performing Arts Center is on the north side, and the Old Market district of shops, boutiques and restaurants lies just to the south. The Leahy Mall is truly a focal point of the modern downtown.

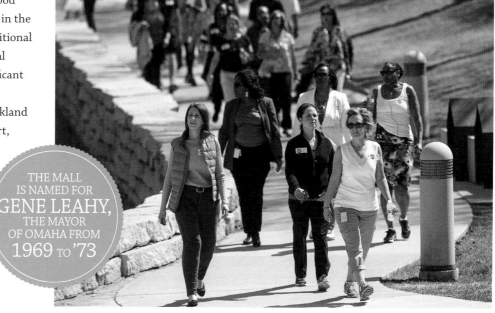

THE MALL IS NAMED FOR **GENE LEAHY,** THE MAYOR OF OMAHA FROM 1969 TO '73

14. BOYS TOWN

IT STARTED OUT nearly a century ago as a home for wayward boys, founded by an immigrant Catholic priest named Father Flanagan. Today it is one of the nation's largest nonprofit child care agencies — its reach and its research extending far beyond Omaha. But Boys Town is synonymous with its hometown.

After becoming famous in a 1938 movie starring Spencer Tracy and Mickey Rooney, Boys Town annually raised millions through letters to donors across the country. But in the beginning, the Rev. Edward Flanagan needed a financial angel — and found one in a Jewish lawyer, Henry Monsky. His role was so crucial that Boys Town considers him one of its founders.

In 1917, the young priest from Ireland borrowed $90 — believed to be from Monsky — to pay the rent on a boarding house that became Father Flanagan's Home for Boys. Four years later, it moved to Overlook Farm west of Omaha, near 144th Street and West Dodge Road. Monsky, who became international president of the Jewish service organization B'nai B'rith, remained a Boys Town supporter and loyal friend of Flanagan. Unfortunately, the pair didn't live to old age. Monsky died at 57 in 1947, and Flanagan at 61 in 1948. But the impact of the two men remains.

Boys Town all along has welcomed children of all races and religions, and in 2011 it elected its first non-Christian board chairman — a Hindu. The home was inclusive and diverse well before those terms came into common usage.

HENRY MONSKY

Considered one of the founders of Boys Town

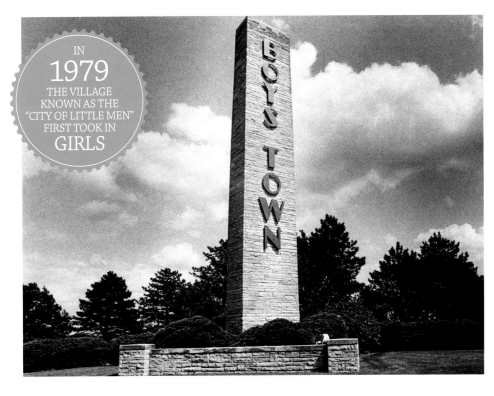

IN **1979** THE VILLAGE KNOWN AS THE "CITY OF LITTLE MEN" FIRST TOOK IN **GIRLS**

"There's no such thing as a bad boy."

— Father Flanagan (above)

The campus includes the famed statue that's the symbol of Boys Town, one boy carrying a younger one on his back and saying, "He ain't heavy, Father; he's my brother."

BOYS TOWN GREETS ABOUT 100,000 VISITORS A YEAR

NATIONAL PRESENCE

Boys Town operates in a dozen cities across the U.S., providing treatment for the behavioral, emotional and physical problems of children and families. Its staffers in Omaha also answer phone calls on a national hot-line. More recently the home has begun placing staff members directly into communities with heavy social needs, including north Omaha and South Omaha.

Omaha long since has grown westward and surrounded the Boys Town campus, which remains a lovely refuge with water, rolling hills and tree-lined streets. The 500 or so youths on the home campus live not in dormitories, as they once did, but in homes led by "family teachers."

Many grads have served in the military, including the late Medal of Honor recipient Vernon Baker. In 1996, he became one of the first seven black Americans — and the only one still living at the time — to receive the medal for service in World War II.

Boys Town enjoys an active alumni association — long-ago grads are referred to as "former boys" — that supports the goal of Catholic canonization of Father Flanagan as a saint. If he is canonized, people will remember that the famed Father Flanagan's Boys Home survived and flourished in the early years because the saintly priest found an angel, a Jewish leader who became his lifelong friend. Legislation to mint a coin commemorating Boys Town's coming 100th anniversary was passed by Congress in 2015.

BOYS TOWN NATIONAL RESEARCH HOSPITAL

Just west of downtown Omaha, the Boys Town National Research Hospital since 1977 has focused on childhood deafness, visual impairment and related communication disorders. The hospital, which includes the Boys Town Ear, Nose and Throat Institute and Boys Town Pediatrics, has been internationally recognized. It serves more than 40,000 children and families across the United States annually.

15. FONTENELLE FOREST

THE FONTENELLES

The forest was named for Logan Fontenelle, and Fontenelle remains a prominent name in the Omaha area because of Fontenelle Forest, the Fontenelle Hills neighborhood and golf course, Fontenelle Park and Fontenelle Boulevard. The Fontenelle Hotel, where presidents, sports stars and others were known to check in before its 1971 closure, was a downtown landmark with its distinctive architecture. A north Omaha housing project, also since torn down, was called the Logan Fontenelle Homes.

So what's the origin of the prominent name? It started with the arrival of Lucien Fontenelle of New Orleans, who ran a fur-trading post and married the daughter of the Omaha chief, Big Elk. They had a son, Logan Fontenelle, who served as an interpreter in negotiations for the Omaha Tribe's surrender of lands in its 1854 treaty with the United States — the year the City of Omaha was founded. Fontenelle Forest and the other Fontenelles are named for him.

"No family in Omaha goes further back."

— Omaha attorney James Cavanaugh, speaking of the Fontenelles

WE'RE A LITTLE SHORT on mountains, but Fontenelle Forest, high above the Missouri River, is a great place to walk and enjoy nature. The Audubon Society reported that 246 species of birds had been recorded there, and Bird Watching magazine said the forest marks a great convergence of eastern and western birds. But there's more to watch than our flying feathered friends.

Deer graze in the deciduous forest, education programs are presented at a nature center and an annual event allows visitors to report the calls of local frogs and toads in the wetlands below, important in helping to conserve amphibians. Flower lovers happily noted in 2014, for the first time since 1975, the emergence of a 4½-foot Turk's cap lily, with a blaze orange and leopard-spotted bloom. The ⅜-mile Gifford Memorial Boardwalk leads to an observation tower over the Great Marsh.

The Lewis and Clark Expedition camped at or near the forest in 1804, and a fur-trading post was founded nearby a few years later, which led to the settlement of Bellevue, the first community in Nebraska. The post eventually was run by French-American trader Lucien Fontenelle of New Orleans. The area later became home to the Bellevue Indian Agency.

A FAVORITE FOR HIKERS

Fontenelle Forest was founded in 1913, and more and more land was acquired over the years. The forest, just south of Omaha, also owns and operates Neale Woods north of the city, donated by a family that had homesteaded the land in the mid-1800s.

16. LAURITZEN GARDENS

THE FIRST IMAGE OF OMAHA for westbound motorists after crossing the Missouri River on Interstate 80 is an urban oasis — Lauritzen Gardens and its $20 million "crystal palace" conservatory. The garden sits high on a bluff above the Missouri River and just north across the highway from the acclaimed Henry Doorly Zoo & Aquarium. How it came about is quite a story.

The vision for the garden dates to 1982, when Helena Street, The World-Herald's garden columnist, invited five people to her home for a discussion. The idea sprouted. In 1996, Spencer Crews, a veteran of the Missouri Botanical Garden in St. Louis and Powell Gardens in Kansas City, was hired in Omaha as executive director. With the help of private donors, a visitor center opened in 2001 and the garden was named for the Lauritzen family, whose forerunners date to Omaha's origins.

New gardens have been added almost every year. In 2005, two old locomotives were mounted on a promontory above I-80, a spot named for John Kenefick, former chairman of another company that helped build Omaha, the Union Pacific Railroad. In 2014, Lauritzen Gardens opened the Marjorie K. Daugherty Conservatory, housing "gardens under glass." Even in the dead of winter, visitors can enjoy something like a tropical heat wave — and see 3,000 non-Nebraska plants among streams, ponds and waterfalls.

FROM TRASH TO TREASURE

In the 1970s, the City of Omaha had implemented a clever idea: trucking daily garbage pickups to a plant north of downtown, where the trash was compacted into bales and moved by rail along the riverfront to be buried in deep ravines. That area now underlies about the northern two-thirds of the botanical garden, which also includes natural woods and rolling terraces.

LAURITZEN GARDENS IS PRIVATELY FUNDED AND OCCUPIES
100 ACRES

"My colleagues are amazed when I talk about a project like this and how the dollars came in. It really is an inspiration."

— Spencer Crews on the financial support received for the "crystal palace" conservatory at Lauritzen Gardens

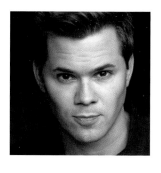

After Omaha native Andrew Rannells was cast in the lead role of Elder Price in Broadway's smash hit "The Book of Mormon," he and his mother visited the Mormon Trail Center in Omaha to soak up history. Rannells, who would win raves for his performance as a perky, perfectionist Mormon missionary in an impoverished Ugandan village, was raised Catholic and graduated from Creighton Prep.

To Latter-day Saints, the actual Book of Mormon is a sacred text. The Broadway version won nine Tony Awards, including best musical. "There's a lot of heart to this story," said Rannells, who also appeared in "The Intern."

"People thought it would be 2½ hours of Mormon bashing, but it's actually a very pro-faith story. It's very funny as well."

17. MORMON TRAIL CENTER

OMAHA IS NO Salt Lake City, but it has its own rich Mormon connection. A Mormon Trail Center, a historic cemetery and a beautiful temple topped by a golden statue of an angel stand together on a hilltop in the Florence area, near the Missouri River. In 2001, the Latter-day Saints faithful opened a temple with a Bethel white granite exterior, rising above the Winter Quarters historic site. A 47-foot spire depicts the Angel Moroni. Before the temple opened, more than 61,000 people were allowed to see it, but then it was closed to all but Mormons in good standing. The Saints consider their temples the holiest sites on Earth, and they use the finest construction materials. The most distinctive feature on the first floor in Omaha is a full-immersion baptistry supported by 12 carved oxen, representing the 12 tribes of Israel. The most sacred rooms are on the second floor, including the celestial room, symbolizing the believer's eternal home in God's kingdom. Church members go there to meditate and pray.

ON THE SITE
IS A SACRED
16,000
SQUARE-FOOT
TEMPLE

A SACRED PLACE

The site commemorates where a pilgrimage paused from 1846 to '48. The Church of Jesus Christ of Latter-Day Saints was founded in 1830 in upstate New York by Joseph Smith, who was killed by a mob in Illinois in 1844. A trek westward stopped in present-day Omaha in 1846 on land belonging to the Omaha Tribe. Several hundred people died from scurvy and exposure, but the Saints established farms to grow sugar beets, turnips and potatoes, and made baskets and washboards to trade for corn, wheat and pork. From that site in 1847, Brigham Young led church members on the 1,000-mile journey to their Promised Land in Utah.

18. EL MUSEO LATINO

EL MUSEO LATINO WAS founded in 1993 by Magdalena Garcia. In honoring her years later, the University of Nebraska at Omaha Alumni Association said she and the museum displayed "the rich canvas of Latino roots and culture."

Much of the Latino community in Omaha, where Latinos now outnumber African-Americans, is centered in South Omaha, not far from the museum at 25th and L Streets. El Museo Latino offers films, lectures, art classes, workshops and dance classes and holds special events throughout the year, including at Cinco de Mayo. The museum's dance company, the Chomari Ballet Folklorico Mexicano, performs lively cultural programs. One of the museum's most high-profile displays was the Smithsonian Institution's 2006 "Our Journeys/Our Stories: Portraits of Latino Achievement."

SOUTH 24TH STREET

Long the Omaha area's "port of entry," South Omaha and the South 24th Street business district have been revitalized in recent decades. Since the 1990s, more and more storefronts have opened with Latino, and a few Asian, names. On residential streets, Hispanic families and others began buying homes of first- and second-generation European immigrants as they died or moved away. South Omaha once was an economic and political hub where power brokers could deliver large blocs of votes and where citywide elections could be won or lost. Now South 24th Street pulses with a Latin beat.

SOUTH 24TH STREET IN AN EARLIER ERA

Previously home to Eastern Europeans, Southern blacks and others who worked in the "Big Four" packinghouses that once made Omaha the nation's largest meatpacking center, South O today looks much different. The giant meatpackers shut down in the 1970s, causing a loss of good-paying jobs. Mainstays like the Philips Department Store eventually closed.

19. OMAHA CHILDREN'S MUSEUM

IT'S CALLED A MUSEUM, but don't picture visitors quietly studying artwork or other exhibits as they stop to read explanatory material. The Omaha Children's Museum, not very quiet, calls itself Omaha's primary participatory museum, where kids not only discover how the world works but also learn through play.

Founded in 1977, the museum at 20th Street and St. Mary's Avenue downtown offers field trips, summer camps, workshops, overnights and birthday parties, and respectfully refers to kids as "our young guests."

The mission is to engage their imagination and create excitement about learning. There's plenty of room for exploring. The museum's 60,000-square-foot size ranks it among the top 15 percent of children's museums worldwide.

THE CHILDREN'S MUSEUM DREW A RECORD 291,000 VISITORS IN 2014

20. GERALD R. FORD BIRTHSITE AND GARDENS

GERALD R. FORD BIRTHPLACE:
3202 WOOLWORTH AVENUE.
THE HOUSE WAS BADLY DAMAGED IN A 1971 FIRE AND WAS RAZED. AFTER FORD BECAME PRESIDENT, IT WAS DISCOVERED TO HAVE BEEN HIS FIRST HOME.
FORD VISITED THE SITE IN 1976.

FORD CONSERVATION CENTER

The Gerald R. Ford Conservation Center (top, left) sits just north of the Ford Birthsite and houses state-of-the-art technical laboratories. Operated by the Nebraska State Historical Society, the center examines and conserves ceramics, glass, metals, photographs, documents, wooden artifacts, works of art on paper and other materials.

THE SITE OF PRESIDENT Gerald R. Ford's original home features a portico that evokes the north side of the White House and a rose garden in memory of first lady Betty Ford.

Born on July 14, 1913, as Leslie King, the future 38th president of the United States lived briefly in a three-story, ornate Victorian house across from the northwest corner of Hanscom Park. His parents divorced and his mother moved with the baby to Grand Rapids, Michigan, where in 1916 she married Gerald R. Ford and renamed her child for him.

In 1974, James M. Paxson, president of Standard Chemical Co. in Omaha and a resident of the neighborhood, bought the property, donated it to the city and set up a foundation to raise funds for a birthsite memorial.

President Ford visited with him at the site in 1976, and it was dedicated in 1977. Ford returned in 1980 for the dedication of the rose garden.

The Gerald R. Ford Expressway, I-480 west of downtown, runs just blocks from the birthsite. (The Ford Presidential Library is in Grand Rapids.)

21. GENERAL DODGE HOUSE

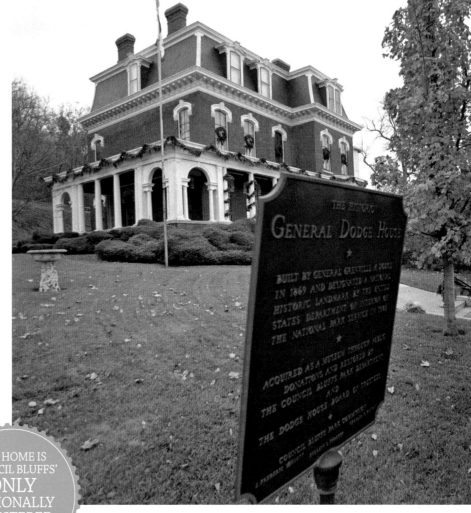

THE HOME IS COUNCIL BLUFFS' ONLY NATIONALLY REGISTERED LANDMARK

THE VICTORIAN-ERA General Dodge House in Council Bluffs, built in 1869 and declared a national historic landmark in 1961, was the home of a man who made a great impact on Abraham Lincoln — and on the development of today's metropolitan area.

Now a museum open to the public, the ornate home was built for Grenville M. Dodge the year the transcontinental railroad was completed. A decade before that, Lincoln and Dodge met on the porch of the appropriately named Pacific House Hotel in the Bluffs (portrayed in the painting at right), and Abe asked for an honest opinion — what's the best route to the Pacific? Replied Dodge: "From this town out the Platte Valley."

Dodge, a Civil War general, railroad builder, congressman and banker, earlier had started the Dodge Land Office in the Bluffs with his brother Nathan, and the N.P. Dodge Co. today remains a full-service real estate firm. Grenville Dodge is not the namesake for Omaha's main east-west street, as many mistakenly believe. The street is named for Augustus Caesar Dodge, a U.S. senator from Iowa.

Lincoln and Gen'l Dodge at Council Bluffs, Aug.1859

A STARTING POINT

That conversation between Lincoln and Dodge helped set the destiny of Omaha, Council Bluffs, Nebraska and the entire nation. Lincoln soon was elected president, and in 1863 he signed the executive order that designated Council Bluffs — and, in effect, Omaha — the terminus for the rail line linking east and west. "That designation," James Potter of the Nebraska Historical Society said in 2009, "had a lot to do with Omaha becoming a metropolis and was a big boost to the economy then and now." People in Omaha and Council Bluffs still debate which city was really the eastern starting point for the rail line. Omaha is the home of the Union Pacific, but both cities have been railroad towns.

BIG NAMES

A prophet is without honor in his own land? Not in Omaha, where we feel a kinship with Omahans — born, raised or still here — who attain national success and celebrity. Their limelight gives us all a nice glow.

22. HOLLYWOOD LEGENDS

OMAHA'S FILM GIANTS

Omahans Marlon Brando, Fred Astaire and Henry Fonda are among the top six actors on the American Film Institute's list of greatest male American screen legends.

1. Humphrey Bogart
2. Cary Grant
3. James Stewart

4. Marlon Brando

5. Fred Astaire

6. Henry Fonda
7. Clark Gable
8. James Cagney
9. Spencer Tracy
10. Charlie Chaplin

THE OMAHA COMMUNITY PLAYHOUSE got its start with folks named Brando and Fonda. Yes, Dorothy Brando, who had a 1-year-old named Marlon, asked her friend Herberta Fonda to nudge son Henry, 20, to try acting with the fledgling theater group. He did so in "You and I" (1925) and received rave reviews for "Merton of the Movies" (1926), before acting on Broadway and becoming a Hollywood legend.

Henry Fonda was Oscar-nominated for "The Grapes of Wrath" in 1940 and won the Academy Award for "On Golden Pond" in 1981, the year before he died at 77. The recipient of many other honors and the patriarch of a family of actors, Fonda never forgot Omaha. He helped to raise money for the Playhouse and appeared at the 1975 reopening of the renovated Orpheum Theater. Its restoration, he said, proved that "to have progress, it's not necessary to tear down the old and build anew." (He also filmed a commercial for Lifesavers candy in the 5100 block of California Street, where he had lived.)

Dorothy Brando and her family left Omaha when Marlon was a toddler, and he grew into a cultural icon and one of America's most influential actors of all time. He was nominated for an Academy Award for "A Streetcar Named Desire" (1951) and won Oscars for "On the Waterfront" (1954) and "The Godfather" (1972). He died in 2004 at 80.

Years later, the names Fonda and Brando remain closely associated with Omaha.

HENRY FONDA WAS A **1923** GRADUATE OF CENTRAL HIGH SCHOOL

DOROTHY BRANDO

Dorothy "Dodie" Brando was herself a star at the Omaha Community Playhouse, playing lead roles in "Pygmalion" and "The Enchanted Cottage." Among Marlon's belongings found when he died was a file of every playbill and review that mentioned his mother's work at the Playhouse.

A LAUNCHING PAD FOR ACTRESSES

The Playhouse also gave a start to Dorothy McGuire, who went from the Omaha stage at 13 (on facing page with Fonda in 1930) to a long career in the movies. McGuire returned to Omaha in 1955 to star with Fonda in "The Country Girl." Making her stage debut in the Playhouse production was 17-year-old Jane Fonda (above and right). "Miss Jane Fonda has a future," The World-Herald's review said. "It may take time, but there is no lack of promise."

DOROTHY MCGUIRE WAS AN ACADEMY AWARD NOMINEE IN
1947
FOR BEST ACTRESS IN "GENTLEMAN'S AGREEMENT"

A STARK CONTRAST: ASTAIRE & BRANDO

A 1998 Time magazine article contrasted Fred Astaire with Marlon Brando, "two fellows from Omaha, Neb., born 25 years apart."

Wrote critic Richard Corliss: "One was frail, comical-looking, yet he epitomized elegance in an era when glamour was the ability to steer a slim lady around a dance floor. The other man was bulky, brooding, with the artistic mission to break things: codes of behavior, the very notion of 'good acting.' In their distinct ways — grace vs. power, gentility vs. menace, tux vs. torn T-shirt — Fred Astaire and Marlon Brando represented the poles of 20th century popular culture. Astaire gave it class; Brando gave it sex.

"These terrific artists also illustrate a pretty little truism about modern culture. In the first half of the century, pop culture imitated the upper class, and in the second half it aped the underclass. Once we gazed on high; now we play limbo with cultural norms. How low can you go?"

FRED ASTAIRE, WHO DANCED ON AIR

How fitting that an Omaha native named Austerlitz kept stepping up his mastery of dance on a stairway to stardom — and became known to the world as Astaire. Yes, Frederick Austerlitz, who lived his early life in a square-framed house at 2326 South 10th Street, became light-stepping Fred-Astaire-who-danced-on-air, a major movie star and perhaps the greatest dancer of the 20th century. As a child, Fred, who attended Kellom School, danced in the ballroom at the Storz Mansion with older sister Adele. (Their father worked at the Storz Brewery.) Their mother took them to New York to start their careers, and they later performed vaudeville at the Orpheum Theater in Omaha. In a scandal-free life marked by modesty, Fred never forgot where he came from. During rehearsals for the 1928 Broadway play "Funny Face," he told its writer he didn't like people knocking his hometown. (Astaire was afraid people would think he was making fun of Omaha, though the lines were harmless. One character asked, "So you were born in Omaha?" The other replied, "No, I was born in a hospital.")

He returned to Omaha a few times over the years, once to accept a Mutual of Omaha award. "I'm sorry to say that I don't get home oftener than I do," he said in 1959. "This is about the first time in, I'd guess, 10 or 15 years. But I get busy with things and can't seem to tear myself away." He died in 1987 at 88.

VISITS HOME

Brando (facing page) sits between mother Dorothy and father Marlon Sr. at the Blackstone Hotel in 1953. Astaire's Omaha cousins Jack, Helene and William Geilus (right) greeted him at Omaha's airport in 1933. Astaire dedicated his autobiography, "Steps in Time," to Helene — and to Omaha.

Omaha "was just right for a hometown — with neighborliness and that small-town feeling without actually being one."

— Fred Astaire on Omaha

PARADE OF STARS

Among the north Omaha athletes who excelled on the biggest stages in sports:

AHMAN GREEN

Omaha Central and Nebraska star is the Green Bay Packers' career rushing leader.

RON BOONE

Omaha Tech grad played in 1,041 consecutive pro basketball games.

ROGER SAYERS

Gale's brother was a world-class sprinter, twice beating the legendary Bob Hayes.

FOR ITS SIZE, OMAHA has produced an outsized number of nationally known African-American athletes — especially those who grew up in a golden era of the 1950s and '60s. Among them from north Omaha were future pros Bob Gibson (baseball), Gale Sayers (football) and Bob Boozer (basketball), as well as Johnny "the Jet" Rodgers, who in 2000 was named the Nebraska Cornhusker football player of the century.

GIBSON PITCHED FOR THE CARDINALS' **OMAHA** FARM CLUB BEFORE STARRING IN ST. LOUIS

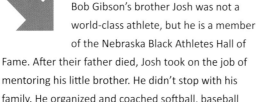

JOSH GIBSON

Bob Gibson's brother Josh was not a world-class athlete, but he is a member of the Nebraska Black Athletes Hall of Fame. After their father died, Josh took on the job of mentoring his little brother. He didn't stop with his family. He organized and coached softball, baseball and basketball teams, mentoring scores of future high school and college stars, including Johnny Rodgers.

BOB GIBSON

Gibson became a Hall of Fame pitcher with the St. Louis Cardinals. As noted in his autobiography, "From Ghetto to Glory," he grew up poor and was mentored by his much older brother Josh. Bob starred at the old Omaha Tech High, earned a basketball scholarship to Creighton University (left) and played for the Harlem Globetrotters before embarking on a 17-year major-league career. His dominance in the 1960s in part led major league baseball to lower the pitcher's mound from 15 inches to 10 inches and tighten the strike zone — moves that were labeled "The Gibson Rules."

GALE SAYERS

Football great Gale Sayers graduated from Omaha Central High and the University of Kansas before electrifying pro football with the Chicago Bears. He scored six touchdowns in a game as a rookie and was acclaimed as the NFL's best open-field runner until a knee injury cut his career short. His friendship with teammate Brian Piccolo led to the TV movie "Brian's Song," based on Sayers' autobiography, "I Am Third." (His credo: "The Lord is first, my friends are second, and I am third.") Sayers became a business leader and philanthropist.

SAYERS, PLAYING FOR KANSAS, SCORED ON A
99-YARD TOUCHDOWN RUN AGAINST NEBRASKA

"In his relatively short career, he compiled a record that can never be forgotten."

— Pro Football Hall of Fame

GALE SAYERS' LONG JUMP RECORD

The Omaha Central star held Nebraska's high school long-jump record for 44 years. His 24-10½ jump finally was surpassed in 2005. Sayers' jump became legendary, in part because of the story behind it. His coach, Frank Smagacz, put a handkerchief in the pit as a target for him to hit, at the time a legal maneuver. Smagacz then kicked it forward about a foot. Sayers landed on it, and in the record book.

BOB BOOZER

Bob Boozer, two years younger than Gibson, played at Tech High and became an All-American at Kansas State before earning a gold medal at the 1960 Olympics and playing 12 years in the NBA, culminating with a championship for the Milwaukee Bucks. He returned to Omaha and the business world before becoming a member of the Nebraska Parole Board.

"I want to say hi to all my friends in Omaha!"

— Boozer, interviewed on national TV immediately after winning an NBA title in 1971 with the Milwaukee Bucks

MARLIN BRISCOE

From South High in Omaha came Marlin "the Magician" Briscoe, who played for Omaha University (now UNO) and then went pro. He holds a distinction in pro football – the first black starting quarterback, in 1968 for the Denver Broncos, then of the American Football League. He later played wide receiver for the Miami Dolphins and was a member of the undefeated 1973 Super Bowl champion team.

JOHNNY RODGERS

Johnny the Jet, another Tech High grad, helped lead Nebraska to national championships in 1970 and 1971. He starred for the Montreal Alouettes of the Canadian Football League for four years, and then played two years with the San Diego Chargers. His pro career, like that of Gale Sayers, ended early with a knee injury. Today the college football award for the best kick returner is named the Jet Award in his honor.

JOHNNY RODGERS' BIGGEST PUNT RETURN

Rodgers is best known for his 72-yard touchdown return against Oklahoma in the 1971 "Game of the Century." College Football News called him "the greatest kick returner in college football history."

COLLEGE FOOTBALL NEWS RANKED HIM NO. 44 ON ITS LIST OF THE 100 GREATEST PLAYERS OF ALL TIME

HEISMAN WINNERS

Omaha has produced three Heisman Trophy winners as the best player in college football.

NILE KINNICK

Omaha Benson graduate Kinnick played at Iowa and won in 1939. He accepted the trophy in New York with an eloquent speech that ended with a powerful line amid the winds of war. "I thank God," the 21-year-old football star said, "that I was warring on the gridirons of the Midwest, and not on the battlefields of Europe." He died in a plane crash in 1943 on a training flight.

JOHNNY RODGERS

Rodgers won in 1972 after helping Nebraska to two national titles. He set NCAA records for all-purpose yardage and punts returned for touchdowns. He was selected to the Walter Camp all-century football team in 1999.

ERIC CROUCH

Millard North product Eric Crouch both rushed and passed for more than 1,000 yards in 2001, his Heisman year. He set an NCAA record for rushing touchdowns by a quarterback with 59 and in one game scored on a run, a pass and a reception.

FIGHTING FOR OTHERS:

"I just like helping people. When I'm coming from nothing and nobody helped me, and I can be in a position to help somebody else, it makes me feel great inside."

— Terence Crawford, who traveled to Africa with his fourth-grade teacher, Jamie Nollette, to help bring clean water to rural Uganda through her Pipeline Worldwide.

24. TERENCE "BUD" CRAWFORD

TERENCE "BUD" CRAWFORD ANSWERS to another name, "Champ." Omaha's first boxing world champion, who has thrilled hometown throngs at the Century-Link Center, claimed titles in the 135- and 140-pound weight classes and was named the all-class 2014 fighter of the year. In 2015, Crawford cracked Ring magazine's Top 10 pound-for-pound ranking of all boxers, and was pictured on the Ring cover.

His reputation growing, Crawford is under contract to Top Rank and has appeared on HBO. In his hometown, he was roasted and toasted at the Omaha Press Club by a panel that included Ron Stander, who fought Joe Frazier in a heavyweight championship fight at the Omaha Civic Auditorium in 1972. That thrilling, sold-out bout, which the popular "Bluffs Butcher" lost on a TKO to Frazier, was matched more than 40 years later when Crawford brought 11,000 screaming fans to their feet at the CenturyLink. In a sensational ninth round, he dropped previously unbeaten Yuriorkis Gamboa four times before the fight was stopped.

Bud Crawford, credited with single-handedly resurrecting interest in boxing in Omaha, surely knows this: His hometown stands firmly in his corner.

THE COMPANY HE KEEPS

Crawford joined select company in being named 2014 fighter of the year. Past winners include Jack Dempsey, Joe Louis, Ray Robinson, Rocky Marciano, Muhammad Ali, Joe Frazier, George Foreman, Sugar Ray Leonard, Thomas Hearns, Marvin Hagler, Mike Tyson, Manny Pacquiao and Floyd Mayweather Jr.

25. ALEXANDER PAYNE

AS A KID IN THE Dundee neighborhood, Alexander Payne made 8 mm movies to show to friends. Now the director-screenwriter owns two Academy Awards, keeps a home in Omaha and enjoys telling Hollywood friends and others about his hometown. In an anthology of the 50 U.S. states, "A Panoramic Portrait of America," Payne penned the chapter on Nebraska. "Visitors are startled," he wrote, "by how cool and modern Omaha seems to be."

Payne's roots run deep. His immigrant grandfather from Greece changed his name from Papadopoulos to Payne to avoid prejudice. The family for years ran the old 24-hour Virginia Cafe downtown on the site of today's main public library. A graduate of Creighton Prep, Stanford and the UCLA film school, Alexander quipped that in his 30s, his father was still offering to pay for law school.

But Alexander's career unfolded in a big way. He filmed "Citizen Ruth" (1996) in Omaha with actress Laura Dern. Reese Witherspoon later said it was "one of the movies that made me want to be an actress." Witherspoon won the lead role in Payne's 1999 film, "Election," set at Papillion La Vista High School. Payne then filmed "About Schmidt" (2002) with Jack Nicholson in Omaha.

Alexander won adapted-screenplay Oscars for "Sideways" (2004) and "The Descendants," (2011) starring George Clooney. Accepting in front of an international TV audience, Payne paid tribute to his mom, Peggy (right). "My mother is here with me from Omaha," he said. "She made me promise if I ever won again that I would dedicate it to her. ... So, Mom, this is for you."

Payne's 2013 black-and-white film, "Nebraska," caused a few letter-writers to accuse him of showing the state as bleak, empty and colorless, and Nebraskans as simpletons. Payne disagreed.

Mark Hoeger, an adjunct professor of film history and appreciation at the University of Nebraska at Omaha, said Nebraska is fortunate to have a native son who makes intelligent comedies. "In a world of sophomoric, bathroom, gross-out humor that has dominated Hollywood comedy," Hoeger said, "it's nice to see a comedy with sophistication and insight."

"I love my state so much that I've devoted most of my professional career to setting stories here and will continue to do so."

— **Alexander Payne, on filming "Nebraska"**

PAYNE'S 1999 FILM, "ELECTION," WAS SET AT PAPILLION LA VISTA HIGH.

PAYNE'S FRIEND TOM WARE

The year that Payne received his second Oscar, a boyhood pal with whom he had ridden bicycles also received national attention. Tom Ware of Ware House Productions in Omaha attended the Grammy Awards because of his nomination for sound engineering on a Lady Gaga album. Payne, who called him "my first best friend," has a second home in California — but never has strayed far from his hometown.

26. JOHNNY CARSON

BEFORE THE QUICK-WITTED Johnny Carson became a legend on late-night TV and part of the national culture, he began his broadcasting career in Omaha — and helped launch television in the Big O. He first got a radio job at WOW. Two months later, on August 29, 1949, he sat in the announcer's booth at WOW-TV for the small screen's Omaha debut. According to one estimate, only 4,000 TV sets existed within a 60-mile radius of Omaha.

Johnny knew enough to be funny, and he was that from the start. Douglas County officials said they wanted to remove pigeons from the roof of the courthouse, so Johnny went there to "interview" the pigeons on radio. With his legs dangling over the edge, he would ask a question and a sound engineer then would play a cooing sound, as if a pigeon were replying. Carson would comically translate. His dual radio-TV gig included hosting a five-day-a-week TV show from 4 p.m. to 5 p.m., "The Squirrel's Nest." (His director was Donald Keough, who became president of Coca-Cola Co.) In a 1984 interview with veteran Omaha cameraman Arlo Grafton, Carson said: "I'm still doing on this show, 'The Tonight Show,' what basically I did in Omaha years ago. This, in essence, is just an expanded version of 'The Squirrel's Nest.'"

He left Omaha near the end of 1951, and hosted "The Tonight Show Starring Johnny Carson" on NBC from 1962 to 1992. He stayed in touch with a few Omaha friends and would arrange seating if they visited his show. An amateur magician, Carson signed off after 30 years and then practically made himself disappear. Marilyn Maye, who often sang in Omaha and appeared on "The Tonight Show" a record (for singers) 76 times, was asked later if she had heard from Johnny. She replied: "Nobody has." Johnny Carson died in 2005.

"I suppose all of us in those days were pioneers in a sense because none of us knew anything about it."

— Johnny Carson, in a 1984 interview

CARSON WAS A 1949 GRADUATE OF THE UNIVERSITY OF NEBRASKA

APPEARING AT AKSARBEN RACETRACK FOR THE JOHNNY CARSON HANDICAP, HE BET ON THE WRONG HORSE. BUT HE MADE MILLIONS ON TV, AND WAS GENEROUS IN DONATING TO CAUSES IN NEBRASKA.

CELEBRITY CHEFS

In 1969, Carson opened an Omaha hamburger restaurant, Here's Johnny's, with the hope that it would become a national chain. The same year, Bob Gibson and Bob Boozer started a chain called Time Out. Carson's chain is gone, but Time Out Foods in north Omaha remains with the original menu.

27. CHIP DAVIS

MANNHEIM STEAMROLLER CHRISTMAS SHOWS TOUR IN TWO COMPANIES — TO A TOTAL OF MORE THAN 75 CITIES.

"MANNHEIM STEAMROLLER" COMES FROM "MANNHEIM CRESCENDO," A GERMAN MUSICAL TECHNIQUE OF THE 1700S

"I love the clean air, the people, the quality of food, everything. It's a great place to raise a family."

—Chip Davis, who never intended to live permanently in the Omaha area but has happily done so.

THE FOUNDER OF GRAMMY Award-winning Mannheim Steamroller, which has sold more than 40 million albums from its base in the middle of America, often is asked why, of all places, he lives in Omaha.

He grew up in a small town in northeast Ohio, his dad a music teacher and his mother a trombonist. At the University of Michigan, Chip focused on classical music, planning to play bassoon in symphonies. In the early '70s he came to Omaha for a workshop, accepted an offer to conduct "Hair" at a dinner theater and promised himself he never would live permanently in Nebraska or write country music. By 27, he was named country music writer of the year. With Bill Fries, Chip had created bread commercials about fictional C.W. McCall and his girlfriend Mavis at the Old Home Fill 'er Up and Keep on Truckin' Cafe. That led to "Convoy," selling 10 million copies and then a movie starring Kris Kristofferson. Chip wasn't really a country-music guy, though, and his greatest work lay ahead — he called it "18th-century classical rock."

Davis released several successful Fresh Aire albums but became famous in 1984 with his first Christmas album and national tour under his own American Gramaphone label — the start of a franchise that made it the biggest-selling Christmas music group of all time. His electronic version of "Deck the Halls" became an instant classic, and the group has played it in two recent Macy's Thanksgiving Day Parades.

'OMAHA'S OWN' ... SORT OF

Omaha likes to proudly claim some other big names, even if they lived here only briefly.

GERALD R. FORD

The 38th president was born Leslie Lynch King Jr. in Omaha in 1913. His mother moved away when he was an infant and remarried.

MALCOLM X

The civil rights activist was born Malcolm Little in Omaha in 1925, but his family moved a year later.

MONTGOMERY CLIFT

The actor, nominated for four Academy Awards, was born in Omaha in 1920 but grew up in New York.

TOM BROKAW

The newsman got his start at KMTV from 1962 to 1965 before rising to the anchor chair on the NBC Nightly News. He lived at the corner of 42nd and Farnam.

WADE BOGGS

The baseball Hall of Famer was born in Omaha in 1958 while his father was stationed at Offutt Air Force Base, but he grew up in Florida.

ANDY RODDICK

The 2003 U.S. Open men's singles champion was born in Omaha in 1982, but his family moved when he was young. His brother was a state diving champion at Creighton Prep.

28. *NAMES TO KNOW IN ENTERTAINMENT*

JOHN BEASLEY

John Beasley, a former Omaha Tech High and Omaha University football player, worked on the railroad for the Union Pacific until starting a remarkable career in his 40s — TV, film and stage actor. He also established the John Beasley Theater and Workshop in South Omaha.

He played a defensive coach in the inspiring 1993 film about a Notre Dame sub, "Rudy," and has appeared in about 25 other movies, including "The Apostle," "The Sum of All Fears" and, in 2015, "Sinister 2." On TV, he played a main role, Irv Harper, in 89 episodes of "Everwood" (2002-2006) and another main role in "The Soul Man" (2012). He also has appeared on shows ranging from "The Untouchables" to "Judging Amy" to "Boston Legal."

When he performed in August Wilson's "Fences" at the Kennedy Center in Washington, D.C., USA Today wrote that Beasley was "by turns hilarious, infuriating and heartbreaking."

GABRIELLE UNION

Gabrielle Union, whose parents and grandparents once worked in packinghouses, became a TV and movie star. Though she left Omaha at 8, Gabrielle has said: "I love Nebraska. I love Cornhusker football. You can't keep me away!" She and husband Dwyane Wade, a pro basketball star, were presented Husker jerseys at the first game at Memorial Stadium in 2015. Union has returned home for Native Omahan Days, and a lagoon in Adams Park is named "Gabrielle Union Pond."

NICHOLAS D'AGOSTO

D'Agosto worked at his father's Arby's restaurant in Omaha while attending Omaha Creighton Prep. His television roles include "Gotham" and "Masters of Sex." He also has appeared in films, including "Final Destination 5" and "Rocket Science."

CHRIS KLEIN

Alexander Payne's "Election" launched the career of Millard West graduate Klein. The film was shot almost entirely in and around Omaha and Papillion using high school students as extras. Klein also has been in "American Pie," "We Were Soldiers" and "Rollerball."

JAIME KING

Omaha Westside graduate King started in modeling before moving to acting and directing. Her films include "Pearl Harbor" and "Sin City." She said she might have starred in "The Notebook" but that there was "no chemistry" with Ryan Gosling during a screen test.

ADAM DEVINE

The Millard South High grad writes and stars in the Comedy Central series he created, "Workaholics." He also appeared in "Pitch Perfect," "Pitch Perfect 2" and "The Intern."

MAURO FIORE

The Omaha cinematographer has worked with Steven Spielberg, Michael Bay, Peter Berg and Joe Carnahan and won an Oscar in 2010 for shooting James Cameron's "Avatar." Fiore also has partnered with director Antoine Fuqua on "Training Day, " "Tears of the Sun " and "The Equalizer."

Fiore brought his statue to his daughters' school and answered questions about Hollywood.

The kids laughed when he admitted to being nervous at the Academy Award ceremony and forgetting to thank his wife during his acceptance speech.

HARRY FRIEDMAN

You could say that Omaha native Harry Friedman, who works in television, followed in his father's footsteps. But there's a difference. His dad sold and repaired some of Omaha's first TVs in the late 1940s and early 1950s. Harry is the executive producer of "Jeopardy," America's No. 1 quiz show, and "Wheel of Fortune," the No. 1 game show.

The 1964 Omaha Central High graduate moved to California in the early 1970s, hoping to get into television. He won his first Emmy at 27, but now those awards number in double figures, which put him in the Guinness Book of World Records. He also received a Peabody Award for meritorious public service and excellence.

NICK NOLTE

Omaha native Nick Nolte has been nominated for three Academy Awards, appeared in dozens of movies and been named People magazine's 1992 "sexiest man alive." Remembered as something of a roustabout in his teens, not always acting right — but in a long career, he certainly has acted well.

He first gained national attention for his 1976 TV role as Tom Jordache in "Rich Man, Poor Man," and followed with his first major film role in "The Deep" in 1977. He later starred with Eddie Murphy in the 1982 buddy cop/convict film, "48 Hrs.," and with Barbra Streisand in the 1991 box-office hit "The Prince of Tides," in which he received a best-actor Oscar nomination. He also received a best-actor nomination for "Affliction" (1997) and a supporting-actor nomination for "Warrior" (2011).

In Omaha, he played football at Benson High but was kicked off the team for drinking and spent his final year as a kicker at Westside, where he also averaged 16 points in basketball. He received a suspended sentence for making fake draft cards, and left town in the early 1960s.

Nolte (center) in 2009 attended the 50th reunion of his Omaha Westside High graduating class. School friends have recalled him as a free spirit who liked to cruise around town, drink beer and play sports.

MIKE HILL

The film editor, an Omaha Burke grad, has worked with director Ron Howard on more than 20 movies, including Oscar- winning best picture "A Beautiful Mind." He won his own Academy Award in 1996 for his work on "Apollo 13."

29. CONNECTIONS

IS OMAHA A SMALL big town, or a big small town? You might think the latter if you listen in when Omahans meet and quickly search for a connection. "What high school did you go to?" is always popular. That might lead to "Isn't she related to ..." Or maybe, "Didn't he used to be ..." It even works with some of Omaha's best-known celebrities. Here's a connection that starts with Bob Gibson and winds its way to a number of famous names:

Didn't he attend the same grade school as ... ?

BOB GIBSON — *Baseball Hall of Famer*

FRED ASTAIRE — *Movie legend*

Wasn't his wife a friend of the wife of ... ?

Didn't he play in the same youth sports leagues as ... ?

WARREN BUFFETT — *Billionaire investor*

JOHNNY RODGERS — *Heisman Trophy winner*

BOB BOOZER — *Basketball Hall of Famer*

MARLIN BRISCOE — *Pro football's first black starting quarterback*

GALE SAYERS — *Football Hall of Famer*

Wasn't his wife's sister married to the uncle of ... ?

Wasn't one of his early investors the father of ... ?

After basketball, didn't he work at Northwestern Bell, which once employed ... ?

Didn't he play football at Omaha University with ... ?

Wasn't he a star high school athlete in Omaha at the same time as ... ?

SWOOSIE KURTZ — *Tony and Emmy Award winner*

ALEXANDER PAYNE — *Academy Award winner*

HENRY FONDA — *Academy Award winner*

JOHN BEASLEY — *TV, stage and film actor and director*

NICK NOLTE — *Academy Award nominee*

Didn't he attend the same high school as ... ?

Didn't he get started at the Omaha Playhouse after being referred by the mother of ... ?

Didn't he play basketball at the same high school as ... ?

JOHN LLOYD YOUNG — *Star of "Jersey Boys"*

CONOR OBERST — *Singer and songwriter*

MARLON BRANDO — *Academy Award winner*

DOROTHY MCGUIRE — *Academy Award nominee*

TERRY KISER — *"Bernie" in "Weekend at Bernie's"*

Didn't he perform at the same children's theater as ... ?

Didn't the Omaha Playhouse also start the career of ... ?

ARTISTRY

As the aptly named Go magazine in The World-Herald attests, Omaha is a community on the go — constantly so. We enjoy the artistry of creative locals and visitors alike, including big names. Theater, art and music abound.

AFTER LIVABILITY.COM GAVE OMAHA a top 10 national ranking for live music, an MTV website gushed even more — naming Omaha one of the world's most up-and-coming cities for music. Read that again: one of the fastest-rising musical cities on Earth. Actually, Omaha long has embraced music and performers. But MTVIggy.com in 2013 listed Omaha No. 2 — say it again — in the world, alongside Kuala Lumpur, Malaysia; Lagos, Nigeria; Santiago, Chile; Athens, Greece; and Barcelona, Spain. The only U.S. city on the list was Omaha. The website cited Omaha's jazz tradition that dates to the 1920s, as well as the current presence of Saddle Creek Records and the independent music "Omaha sound." Throughout the Omaha area on many nights, it's easy to find live music performances — acoustic, alternative, blues, country, folk, funk, hip-hop, indie, jazz, oldies, reggae, rock, soul and on and on. Not to mention the Omaha Symphony at the Holland Performing Arts Center and national acts at the CenturyLink Center and the Orpheum.

LAUNCHING THE OMAHA SOUND

The nationally known rock band 311, which helped create the "Omaha sound" phenomenon, celebrated its 25th anniversary in 2015 with a concert back where it all began — at the Sokol Auditorium. "It was a really great launching point," recalled frontman Nick Hexum. "And then we just kept building from there."

Hexum and Omaha Westside High classmates Tim Mahoney and Chad Sexton join with Aaron "P-Nut" Willis and Doug "S.A." Martinez, who attended Bryan High, to make up 311, pronounced three-eleven. In the "lean times" of the early 1990s, the band's touring RV caught fire and exploded on the shoulder of a highway, destroying its equipment, clothes, money and personal possessions.

The band members, who suffered minor injuries, persevered. They have enjoyed a successful career playing alternative, reggae, rap and funk rock, with hits such as "Amber" and "Down," and have traveled widely. The band celebrates March 11 with an extended concert on what it has dubbed 311 Day.

The band's name? An early guitarist was arrested for streaking, and 311 was the police code for indecent exposure.

"PERHAPS THE **MOST VITAL UNDERGROUND ROCK SCENE** IN THE COUNTRY"
— New York Times, March 2003

CONOR OBERST

Practically as soon as young singer-songwriter Conor Oberst of Omaha hit the national music scene, some called him the next Bob Dylan. Even as a teenager, the local kid's angst-filled, poetic lyrics struck a chord. Now in his mid-30s, Oberst (left and below) still tours nationally and has sustained a career that includes Rolling Stone magazine naming him the best songwriter of 2008.

The youngest of three sons of a Mutual of Omaha information manager and a school principal, Conor was just 13 when a World-Herald reviewer lauded him as a stage natural in "an astonishingly good performance" in a dinner theater play. By 14, not yet in high school, he was known and respected in Omaha's acoustic music circles. "The adolescent crack of Conor Oberst's singing voice," our entertainment columnist wrote, "belies the strength of the voice within."

Two years later, Oberst recorded in New York, noted as a musical free spirit and for his "acoustic-fed folk with a punk-rock attitude." He appeared on David Letterman's TV show and has sung in front of thousands at California's Coachella music festival and elsewhere. One of Omaha's top musical influences, Oberst had launched his career in the 1990s at the since-closed Cog Factory on Leavenworth Street near downtown Omaha — a place that helped shape Omaha's reputation as a music city.

The greatest strength of the Omaha scene "isn't its sincerity but its skepticism and penchant for self-criticism."

— **New York Times, 2003**

SADDLE CREEK RECORDS & SLOWDOWN

Across the country more than a decade ago, young music fans began talking about "the Omaha sound," the independent music scene spawned here by Saddle Creek Records and others. The New York Times marveled at the music style's rise and tried to answer its own question: "Why Omaha? The Omaha scene is a happy accident. It's what happens when a bunch of great songwriters and musicians find themselves in the same place at the same time."

Musicians such as Tim Kasher and Conor Oberst led the way, but many contributed, including Jason Kulbel and Robb Nansel, whose Saddle Creek became the flagship label of the Omaha style of indie music. The name of the label comes from Saddle Creek Road, which cuts through a mature neighborhood of tree-lined streets.

In 2007, Kulbel and Nansel opened the Slowdown live-music venue in north downtown with a concert by Oberst and his band, Bright Eyes.

WHY THE NAME SLOWDOWN?

The venue is named for an early Omaha-scene band, Slowdown Virginia (below), which became Kasher's popular Cursive.

"Buried deep in the Midwest, Omaha has a thriving and intermingled folk and punk scene, untroubled by what is and isn't cool in distant New York and Los Angeles."

— Daily Telegraph of London

ARC STUDIOS

ARC isn't just "another recording studio," even though its initials came from that phrase. Operated by Mike Mogis (above) of the group Bright Eyes, ARC has attracted musicians from far and wide to record in Omaha, some of whom stay at the studio's adjacent guest house in the burgeoning Benson entertainment district.

Among them: Swedish folk duo First Aid Kit, who had met Mogis and Omaha singer Conor Oberst at a Monsters of Folk concert in Stockholm. The two women stayed next door to ARC while recording their album, "The Lion's Roar." The Philadelphia folk band Good Old War also recorded at ARC and hung out in Dundee at the Amsterdam Falafel & Kabob.

SOKOL AUDITORIUM

Sometimes opposites co-exist. At the Sokol Auditorium, you'll see the 11-piece Jimmy B Orchestra play songs such as "Moonlight Serenade" and "Tennessee Waltz" for ballroom dancing upstairs, while downstairs at the venue's appropriately named Underground, heavy-metal bands do sound checks for that night's concert. Said singer Alex Good, 20, as he surveyed his dancing elders: "This is something you don't see at our gigs. I can't dance like that." Sokol Auditorium, just south of downtown, is one of many venues for live music, and the site of one of Omaha's most unusual events: the February 2 Groundhog Prom, with attendees wearing bizarre costumes in a send-up of the glitzy Aksarben Coronation and Scholarship Ball.

31. MAHA MUSIC FESTIVAL

SEVEN THOUSAND OR MORE music fans from Omaha and around the country gather each August for the all-day, nonprofit Maha Music Festival. Celebrating indie music, food, art and sun, Maha was started by young Omaha professionals who believed their "blossoming, creative community," which contributes "a generous helping of arts, ideas and innovation," needed its own music festival.

The festival is held at Stinson Park on the grounds of the former Ak-Sar-Ben racetrack, and it attracts local as well as nationally known bands. Organizers say they want to push beyond the parameters of traditional music festivals and continue to attract fans from across the U.S., "while celebrating the local community — the people and what they do, what they create and build, and the causes they champion."

MAHA MUSIC FESTIVAL STARTED IN **2009** ON THE RIVERFRONT BUT MOVED TO STINSON PARK

THE PLAYHOUSE IS THE **LARGEST** COMMUNITY THEATER IN THE U.S.

32. OMAHA COMMUNITY PLAYHOUSE

AFTER 90 YEARS OF staging productions almost exclusively with non-professional actors, the Playhouse enjoys a national reputation. Along the way, the theater endured financial stumbles and survived a tornado, expanding its facility so much that it can show two plays at once and have a third in rehearsal — with plenty of space for sets, classes and costuming. Omaha is a strong theater town, with more than a dozen smaller venues, the outdoor Shakespeare on the Green and regular stops at the Orpheum downtown by Broadway touring shows. Competition for entertainment dollars is fierce. The Playhouse competes by staging relevant, edgier works in its smaller theater and endeavoring to fill the seats for its main stage with popular shows. It has benefited from legions of behind-the-scenes volunteers and a foundation that keeps it financially strong.

The arrival of Charles Jones as artistic director and James Othuse as set designer in 1974 proved to be a watershed. Jones created the Playhouse's professional arm, the Nebraska Theatre Caravan, which annually takes the Christmas show on two simultaneous tours. The caravan also produces other plays and musicals.

JANE FONDA RETURNS FOR A VISIT

Jane Fonda (above and below) toured the Playhouse in 2012 with son Troy Garity, actress Laura Dern and director Alexander Payne.

Fonda made her stage debut in a Playhouse production with father Henry Fonda, in 1955. "Dad would be so proud!" she exclaimed as she entered a large, overflowing costume department. "It's like the old movie studios."

AN OMAHA CHRISTMAS CLASSIC

Jones created a musical version of a famous play by another Charles — Dickens. Not only has that adaptation of "A Christmas Carol" filled the house in Omaha each holiday season, providing needed revenue, but it also sends out two annual national tours.

SPECIAL EFFECTS

For decades, the Omaha Community Playhouse has used its onstage trapdoor to great effect to scare the Dickens out of attendees at "A Christmas Carol." As a bell ominously tolls, Ebenezer Scrooge's late partner, Jacob Marley, rises through the floor on an unseen hydraulic lift, amid billowing smoke and green lighting. Looking rather grave, he returns from the crypt to urge Scrooge to mend his miserly, bah-humbug ways. "Woe is me-e-e-e!" Marley's Ghost intones, his amplified voice echoing. "I wear the chain I forged in life." In a two-hour show, the scene lasts a mere seven minutes — but it's a great seven minutes.

"It's an actor's dream to play a part like this that's so far out, and to which the audience always responds."

— Al DiMauro, who played Marley's Ghost for 20 years

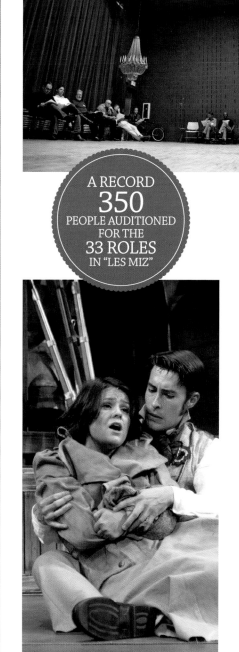

A RECORD **350** PEOPLE AUDITIONED FOR THE **33 ROLES** IN "LES MIZ"

STRONG LOCAL TALENT

Except for bringing in an occasional professional for a major role, such as that of Jean Valjean in "Les Miserables," the Omaha Community Playhouse has relied on talented local folks. Joseph T. O'Connor II (left) performed a major role in the 2013 Playhouse production of "Les Miserables," the most expensive in the theater's history. By day a sewer inspector with leading-man looks, Joe by night sang the role of Marius, whose life is saved — in a sewer.

THE PLAYHOUSE MOVED FROM 40TH & DAVENPORT STREETS TO 69TH & CASS STREETS IN **1959**

MISHAPS & MALFUNCTIONS

- Jill Anderson dashed to the wings as dancers came on. Costumers were helping her get out of a costume, but a zipper stuck and wouldn't budge. "Rip it!" Jill said, and they did. She made a quick change and returned to the stage only seconds late.

- Laura Marr's hair caught on fire, but she beat it out.

- Eric Griffith got a bloody head cut from free-hanging scenery, and the show paused while he was bandaged. When action resumed, his actual next line was coincidentally perfect: "Sorry I'm late. I had a special session with my psychia — er, my head doctor."

55

33. HOLLAND PERFORMING ARTS CENTER

THE $100 MILLION-PLUS Holland Performing Arts Center has received almost universal praise since it opened in 2005, and not just from Omahans. The venue has been hailed by visitors and critics, some of whom sounded a bit surprised.

The Dallas Morning News said the "classy new concert hall complex" was "an essay in crisp, urban modernism" of the kind you might find in Lucerne, Switzerland. The Swiss might poke holes in that comparison, but the Dallas paper's music critic added: "Omaha now has one of the country's best-sounding new concert halls."

The Chicago Tribune raved about "the stunning, glass-wrapped Holland Performing Arts Center," and the American Record Guide said "arts-conscious Omaha" regarded the Holland as an icon. The Architectural Record used that same word, praising the Holland Center's "rich sound, excellent sight lines and striking interior."

HOME TO WORLD-CLASS ARTS & ENTERTAINMENT

The Holland Center is home to the Omaha Symphony, which previously played at the downtown Orpheum Theater. The Holland, designed in a "shoebox" configuration for better acoustics, has welcomed top entertainers such as Wynton Marsalis, Yo-Yo Ma, Tony Bennett, Zoë Keating, Herbie Hancock and the Mormon Tabernacle Choir.

NAMED FOR PRIMARY DONORS RICHARD AND MARY HOLLAND, THE BUILDING INCLUDES A 2,000-SEAT MAIN HALL, 450-SEAT RECITAL HALL AND 10,000-SQUARE-FOOT COURTYARD, AND SITS ALONGSIDE THE TREE-LINED GENE LEAHY MALL AND LAGOON.

MAESTRO THOMAS WILKINS

The conductor of the Omaha Symphony since 2005 jokes that his talent for flapping his arms came from his father — who waved his arms to help pilots park commercial airliners. Maestro Thomas Wilkins spends a lot of time at airports, but not on the tarmac. Though Omaha is home, he flies around the country, much in demand to conduct other symphonies.

Wilkins grew up in a Norfolk, Virginia, housing project known for drug deals and robberies, but after hearing the local symphony, he signed up for violin lessons at public school. He later earned a master's degree in conducting from Boston's New England Conservatory and became conductor of the Detroit Symphony before taking the job in Omaha the year the symphony moved to the new Holland Performing Arts Center.

Wilkins is the 11th music director of the Omaha Symphony, founded in 1921. He also is the principal guest conductor of the Hollywood Bowl Orchestra, has conducted the Philadelphia Orchestra in a Martin Luther King Day tribute and became the first African-American conductor in the 134-year history of the Boston Symphony, leading youth and family concerts. The Boston Globe called him "a burst of energy at graying Symphony Hall. In other words, your grandfather's conductor he is not."

"I now find myself in front of some of the world's greatest orchestras," Wilkins said, "and I juxtapose that to my beginnings. It allows me to stay humble and always grateful, and it informs my work ethic."

"When friends come to town from Los Angeles, Boston or wherever, they walk on that stage for the first time, look around and go, 'Holy smokes!' I just give a nice, proud smile and say, 'Yeah. I know.'"

— Wilkins, who loves showing off the Holland to visiting professionals

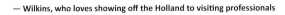

RACHEL JACOBSON

The nonprofit Film Streams, the film dream of Omaha native Rachel Jacobson, became reality in 2007. She was just 28, but the genesis came while she was growing up near Memorial Park, developing her love of film as an art form. After college, she moved to New York, taking courses and jobs to prepare for opening an independent-film theater. Then late one night she walked through Manhattan's East Village with another young Omaha visionary, Robb Nansel of Saddle Creek Records. He explained his idea for a music venue, warehouse and headquarters, and she outlined hers for a film house. Later, when Saddle Creek decided to build Slowdown back home, Robb asked Rachel if she would like to attach her theater. She said yes, set up a nonprofit corporation and raised money — with the support of movie director Alexander Payne of Omaha, now a two-time Oscar winner.

34. FILM STREAMS

"I hate to say this, but even Hollywood doesn't have this, which is truly shameful."

— Jane Fonda, writing in her blog after she visited Film Streams

ARTICLES IN NEW YORK, Chicago or elsewhere that have reported on Omaha's "cultural awakening" always mention Film Streams, the art movie house in north downtown. Film Streams' Ruth Sokolof Theater features a comprehensive array of first-run independent, documentary and foreign films, as well as classic and themed repertory selections and educational programs. In addition, Film Streams works with nonprofits to publicly screen films that are followed by panel discussions. The theater also shows musical performances and silent movies, celebrates the work of artists at a Local Filmmakers Showcase and annually brings in a nationally known figure for a public Q&A session about movies. The name of the movie house was inspired by the film "Love Streams," the theme of which is that love is a universal connector. Founder Rachel Jacobson says movies are, too.

FILMS STREAMS' RUTH SOKOLOF THEATER HAS **TWO SCREENS** SEATING **206 & 96**

FILM STREAMS ALSO PRESENTS LIVE **METROPOLITAN OPERA** PERFORMANCES ON ITS SCREENS

35. LIVE THEATER SCENE

OMAHA IS FORTUNATE TO enjoy "an incredibly vibrant community theater scene," as longtime World-Herald reviewer Bob Fischbach wrote when he retired in 2015. In addition to the Omaha Community Playhouse, numerous small theaters give Omahans plenty of chances to take in live performances.

SHAKESPEARE ON THE GREEN

For three decades, Omahans and visitors from around the country have set down blankets on the sloping landscape at Elmwood Park on dreamy midsummer nights to enjoy Shakespeare on the Green. More than 20,000 attend each year on the greensward in Omaha, up to 5,000 on some nights. They revel in Will's words and his understanding of human nature as well as in the acting of professionals. It's just fun, too, with pre-show jugglers, picnics and wine. It has been a "first date" for some, and one theatrical couple married there in Elizabethan costumes. When a golfer badly hooked a drive from the adjacent course before one show, the ball conked a man on the head. He wasn't seriously injured, but a friend who didn't see what happened wondered how the gazpacho got spilled on top of his noggin. Uh, he was bleeding.

Admission is free, though donations are accepted. Occasionally, the skies open. One year on opening night, after a hard rain, actors performed in the nearby Weber Fine Arts Building at the University of Nebraska at Omaha. They showed that the bad weather was like the name of their play, "Much Ado About Nothing."

THE ORPHEUM THEATER

The ornate splendor of the renovated Orpheum Theater remains beloved in Omaha, and it is home to Broadway touring shows, Opera Omaha and other productions. It is managed by the nonprofit Omaha Performing Arts, which also runs the Holland Performing Arts Center and the summer Jazz on the Green series at Midtown Crossing.

Built in 1927 during the heyday of vaudeville, the Orpheum thrived for its first two decades but transitioned into a movie house and then closed in 1971. The philanthropic Knights of Aksarben purchased and restored it, and the 1975 reopening was headlined by comedian Red Skelton, with an appearance by former Omahan Henry Fonda.

THE ROSE THEATER

One of Omaha's most remarkable structures was vacant and the possible target of a wrecking ball until Rose Blumkin, founder of the Nebraska Furniture Mart, came to the rescue. Since restored, "The Rose" today is a vibrant, busy theater for young people and families.

Opened in 1927 at 20th and Farnam Streets as the Riviera, a grand movie palace, the lavish decor included tapestries, sculptures and friezes, as well as fountains and an intricate mosaic floor. After the stock market crash of '29, the building was sold and became the Paramount. Besides showing movies, the structure was used at times for miniature golf and bowling, and during the space exploration of the 1960s was renamed the Astro Theater. It eventually went unused for a decade, until Blumkin bought the building in 1981. She donated the first $1 million toward renovation and deeded it to the Omaha Theater for Young People.

The company provides classes in theater, directing, musical theater, singing, dancing and more.

BLUE BARN

The first non-university theater to be built in Omaha since 1986 opened in 2015, the indoor-outdoor Blue Barn at 10th and Pacific Streets. The theater, which in recent years produced plays in rented Old Market space, was founded in 1989 by three actors fresh out of college near New York City. They settled in Omaha and began staging cutting-edge, thought-provoking plays. A $7 million capital campaign allowed construction of the new theater in the city's historic Little Italy neighborhood, just south of downtown.

36. BEMIS CENTER AND HOT SHOPS

TWO PLACES HELPING to foster the city's growing artistic reputation are the Bemis Center for Contemporary Arts and the Hot Shops Art Center.

The Bemis Center, in a former grocery warehouse in the Old Market, has hosted more than 700 artists in residence in the past three decades. With an urban garden for sculpture and ceramics as well as exhibition and work space, the Bemis says it serves as a laboratory for artists at the leading edge of their disciplines. The residence program provides time to "research, experiment and take creative risks" so that artists may become "vibrant social, cultural and economic transformers."

The Hot Shops, in a former mattress factory in north downtown, includes 50 art studios, four art galleries and various exhibition spaces. On any given day, ovens may bake clay and furnaces may melt metal in one building while people in studios next door paint, sculpt, draw, design or make photographs.

In addition to the Bemis and the Hot Shops, the nonprofit Omaha Creative Institute supports artists and strengthens an appreciation of art in the Omaha area through hands-on creative workshops and other initiatives. Local artists teach origami, cartooning, blacksmithing, photography, painting, beginning ukulele and more.

The artistic landscape of Omaha is "always charged and changing." — The Artist's Magazine

HOT SHOPS ART CENTER GOT ITS NAME FROM THE **KILNS AND FURNACES** USED BY ITS FOUNDING MEMBERS

37. JUN KANEKO

OMAHA'S RESURGENCE IN RECENT decades as a rising, creative city has coincided with its hometown connection to internationally acclaimed artist and sculptor Jun Kaneko (k'neck-o). A native of Japan, Kaneko creates giant ceramic sculptures that are shown around the world and designs living, breathing sets for opera that are made of — lighting.

In addition, he and wife Ree in 2008 opened a nonprofit Omaha center of creativity in an Old Market warehouse, called simply "Kaneko." It offers programs of many kinds and provides ample space for lectures, meetings and gallery display in a setting known as "open space for the mind."

In the late 1980s, Jun Kaneko moved to Omaha, his wife's home, and has made a global impact from the Old Market district downtown. That's where the couple live, and it's home to his kiln and studio.

Jun thinks big, which he calls "the spiritual scale," making the viewer one with the art. He creates colorful Easter Island-like Heads, as well as cylindrical Dangos (Japanese for dumplings) and Tanukis, which are raccoon dogs popular in folktales. Cute, yes, but also 7 feet tall and weighing 900 pounds.

Each piece takes great time and effort, he says, and had better be good. He quipped, "So don't make ugly, big piece!"

DESIGNING FOR THE STAGE

In recent years, Kaneko also has turned his talents to opera. He has designed three, starting with Opera Omaha's "Madama Butterfly," and then the San Francisco Opera's production of Mozart's "The Magic Flute," which also was shown in Omaha. He also designed Beethoven's "Fidelio" for Opera Philadelphia, which later was performed at the Orpheum in Omaha (above).

BORN IN 1942, KANEKO CAME TO AMERICA AT 21 TO STUDY **PAINTING** BUT TURNED TO **CERAMICS**

KANEKO'S ART ALSO HAS BEEN SHOWN IN **NEW YORK & CHICAGO**, WITH A 2016 EXHIBIT IN **TOKYO**

38. BIG-NAME ENTERTAINMENT

A FOCAL POINT of today's lively Omaha is our riverfront convention center and arena, a draw for big-name entertainers. The CenturyLink Center has hosted Paul McCartney, Lady Gaga, Justin Timberlake, Taylor Swift, Bruce Springsteen, Elton John, Janet Jackson, the Rolling Stones and many others. The arena ranked No. 78 in the world with 185,069 tickets sold in 2014.

A SIX-CONCERT VISIT IN MAY 2015 BY COUNTRY SINGER **GARTH BROOKS DREW ABOUT 100,000 FANS.**

A LONG TIME COMING

For decades, the city had considered replacing the 1955 Civic Auditorium with a new convention center — idea after idea, plan after plan, study after study. The topic was practically studied to death. The convention center-arena bond issue approved by voters in 2000 was for $198 million, with another $75 million contributed by wealthy Omahans, and several million more coming from other sources. The convention center has had its share of big names, too, serving as host to fundraising banquets and meetings that included speeches by Barack Obama, Archbishop Desmond Tutu and three Clintons: Bill, Hillary and Chelsea. When civic leaders started dreaming of riverfront development in the 1970s, the CenturyLink Center is something like what they imagined. Now it's hard to imagine Omaha without it.

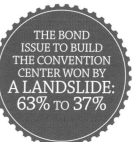

THE BOND ISSUE TO BUILD THE CONVENTION CENTER WON BY **A LANDSLIDE: 63% TO 37%**

39. LOVE'S JAZZ & ARTS CENTER

LOVE'S JAZZ & ARTS CENTER near 24th and Lake Streets honors the memory of the late Omaha musician Preston Love. The African-American cultural and jazz center features the Preston Love gallery, exhibition space, a gift shop, classrooms and a performing arts area.

HOME BASE

Love returned to Omaha in 1971, although he continued to tour. He wrote that Count Basie "always seemed to enjoy having 'the kid from Omaha' so totally consumed by the worship of him."

"People in the African-American community have stories to tell, and if we don't tell them ourselves, in a place like this, who will?"

— The late jazz great Luigi Waites, who performed with his band at Love's Jazz & Arts Center

PRESTON LOVE

- Born in Omaha in 1921, his career began at age 15 with a gig in Honey Creek, Iowa.

- In 1938, he was inspired upon hearing Earle Warren playing in the Count Basie Orchestra. He replaced Warren as lead alto saxophonist in Basie's band in the 1940s.

- In the 1950s, he led his own band, and in 1952 he launched the short-lived Spin Records.

- In the 1960s and 1970s, he directed the West Coast Motown Orchestra, which backed singers like Ray Charles, Diana Ross, Marvin Gaye and Stevie Wonder and toured with the Temptations and Four Tops.

- His love of the Midwest brought him back to Omaha, where he played local gigs while continuing national tours and frequent trips to Europe. Love became a tireless advocate for jazz and rhythm and blues, and their history in Omaha and Kansas City. He died in 2004.

40. "FERTILE GROUND"

"I've worked on a lot of murals. I've never seen anything like this. We've had scores of volunteers put in thousands of hours. It's really amazing."

— Meg Saligman, the mural's internationally renowned, Philadelphia-based artist

A NATIONAL PUBLICATION, The Artist's Magazine, hailed Omaha as a paradise for artists — an always changing landscape of eccentric and beautiful locales amid people who appreciate artists.

Omaha supports the arts in a big way. At about 75 feet high and a football field long, a mural on the exterior wall of the former Energy Systems Inc. building in north downtown has been called monumental and gigantic. Not to mention striking and beautiful.

Across 13th Street from TD Ameritrade Park and in view of the CenturyLink Center, the mural depicts 46 Omahans past and present. Among them are construction magnate Peter Kiewit, jazz musician Preston Love (both deceased) and a composite of a dancing woman reaching for the sky to symbolize Omaha's future and potential.

The Peter Kiewit Foundation — which also has supported the creation of sculptures outside the CenturyLink convention center and arena and other public art — commissioned the mural to foster civic pride. Many businesses and individuals jumped in to help, and the Bemis Center for Contemporary Arts directed the project, which was completed in 2009. All the folks with fertile imaginations who made the "Fertile Ground" mural a reality merit applause, a cheer and a beer.

EVENTS

Why do Omahans go crazy over big events? Without top-level pro sports, not to mention mountains or beaches, we are drawn to what gives us a little national attention. Truth to tell, we enjoy our moments in the sun.

41. COLLEGE WORLD SERIES

IT'S BEEN CALLED our own Kentucky Derby or Indianapolis 500, a near-fortnight each June when the national sports focus is on Omaha. The eight-team national baseball tournament is unique among NCAA championships because no other locale has permanently hosted an event for anything like the 60-plus years the CWS has unfolded in the Big O. Other cities have sought to lure it away, but Omaha has fought off the suitors. In return for a 25-year NCAA contract to keep the series, Omaha (through donations and visitor taxes) built the $128 million TD Ameritrade Park, which opened downtown in 2011. Jim Hendry, former Creighton coach who became general manager of the Chicago Cubs, called it America's best ballpark outside the major leagues. The games are televised by ESPN, which never fails to augment the broadcasts with lovely views of Omaha.

HOW IT BEGAN

The College World Series belongs to the NCAA, but the CWS has flourished in part because of the strong working relationship with the nonprofit College World Series of Omaha Inc., which was created in 1967 by the late John Diesing (below). The leadership has since passed to his son, John "Jack" Diesing Jr. The first two series were played in Kalamazoo, Michigan. After Wichita, Kansas, hosted in 1949, the NCAA and college baseball coaches searched for a new city. Omaha put in the winning bid in 1950, and the city warmly embraced the event.

REMEMBERING ROSENBLATT

Omahans still speak fondly of Rosenblatt Stadium. Moving to TD Ameritrade Park was a bittersweet, controversial decision, because it meant abandoning the beloved Rosenblatt, home of the CWS since 1950. That "diamond on the hill," built in 1948 as Municipal Stadium, was renamed in 1964 for Johnny Rosenblatt, a popular former Omaha mayor who had played semipro ball. It also was the home for Class AAA professional baseball, including the Kansas City-affiliated Omaha Royals (briefly called the Golden Spikes) from 1969 to 2010.

A mile and a half south of downtown, "The 'Blatt" sat next to the Henry Doorly Zoo on a bluff high above the Missouri River. The charm of Rosenblatt, which one coach characterized as a "county fair atmosphere," included Lambert Bartak on the organ and public-address announcer Jack Payne encouraging folks in the bleachers to "scooch together" so more fans could get in. The umpires once danced the Hokey Pokey between innings, and an impromptu RV camp sprang up outside called "Dingerville" for the LSU fan who started it, Glenarp Allmendinger. But the NCAA eventually wanted a modern park with more room for sponsored events outside the stadium.

ROSENBLATT'S SINGLE-GAME ATTENDANCE RECORD:
30,553 FANS

A HOMETOWN WELCOME

Omaha has cherished the CWS all along, warmly welcoming visiting teams and assigning local service clubs to make sure every need is taken care of off the field. Teams are treated like royalty, bused from their hotels to the stadium with a lights-flashing police escort.

But the city received a special thrill in 1991 when the hometown Creighton Bluejays (above), their campus three miles from Rosenblatt Stadium, traveled 1,500 miles to Los Angeles to win an NCAA regional and qualify for the College World Series. Fans turned out even for batting practice, chanting "Bluejays! Bluejays!" The potent Jays, with the nation's top team batting average, were no fluke — they won two games and finished third in the nation.

THE NEBRASKA CORNHUSKERS, FROM 50 MILES AWAY IN LINCOLN, DREW STRONG LOCAL SUPPORT WHEN THEY PLAYED IN THE CWS IN 2001, 2002 AND 2005.

CWS FUTURE STARS

1973
DAVE WINFIELD
Minnesota

1977
PAUL MOLITOR
Minnesota

1983
ROGER CLEMENS
Texas

1985
WILL CLARK
Mississippi State

1984
BARRY BONDS
Arizona State

1987
ALBERT BELLE
Louisiana State

1990
MIKE MUSSINA
Stanford

1994
JASON VARITEK
Georgia Tech

1995
TODD HELTON
Tennessee

1997
LANCE BERKMAN
Rice

2005
ALEX GORDON
Nebraska

2008
BUSTER POSEY
Florida State

THE PLACE TO CATCH A RISING STAR

For Omahans, one of the CWS's main attractions is getting a chance to say, "I saw him when he played for ... " The list of CWS alums includes Hall of Famers, major league All-Stars and No. 1 draft picks. Dave Winfield (above) in 2013 was named to the Omaha College World Series Hall of Fame. Winfield, who was a three-sport athlete at the University of Minnesota, pitched his way to the most outstanding player award in the 1973 College World Series. Drafted in the first round by the San Diego Padres, Winfield made his first professional start without any time in the minor leagues. His résumé after 22 years as a major league outfielder included 3,110 hits, 465 home runs, 12 All-Star appearances, seven Gold Gloves and a World Series trophy.

KYLE PETERSON

Kyle Peterson (right) grew up in Omaha attending College World Series games. He eventually was thrilled to pitch in the CWS and then became a TV commentator. World-Herald columnist Tom Shatel called him "Mr. College Baseball, a perfect ambassador for Omaha and the game he broadcasts on ESPN."

Peterson and his Creighton Prep teammates won a state championship at Rosenblatt Stadium, and he returned there in 1995 to pitch for Stanford University in the CWS. He later pitched in the major leagues for the Milwaukee Brewers before becoming CEO of Colliers International, an Omaha commercial real estate firm. But for years he has continued to broadcast college baseball, traveling the country each spring and coming home to Omaha for the eight-team national championship series, now at TD Ameritrade Park. He was critical of the NCAA for allowing offense to decline but praised it for changes — including a lower-seam ball with less drag as it flies toward the fences.

His personal favorite CWS memory was hearing the longtime PA announcer say his name. "I heard Jack Payne say so many names growing up. To hear him say my name was a highlight."

42. COLLEGE HOME RUN DERBY & FIREWORKS

TD AMERITRADE PARK ALSO IS host to the College Home Run Derby.
The event, which features eight of college baseball's best sluggers, has been
coupled with the Omaha World-Herald Independence Day fireworks show
since the ballpark opened in 2011. The event draws more than 20,000 to
the stadium and tens of thousands more outside the ballpark. The annual
World-Herald fireworks night started in 1985 and for years was centered
at Rosenblatt Stadium. People who couldn't get in filled nearby parks,
yards and sidewalks all around, with some estimates rising to 150,000.

30,000 SHELLS WERE LAUNCHED DURING THE **22-MINUTE** SHOW IN 2015

43. BIG SPORTING EVENTS

OLYMPIC SWIM TRIALS

Omaha loves ball sports, but swimming? Yes, as it turned out, and now the U.S. Olympic Swim Trials will be held at the CenturyLink Center downtown in 2016, the third Olympiad in a row. Getting to host the Trials the first time in 2008 was a coup. But the sport's national governing body, USA Swimming, realized from Omaha's longtime love of the College World Series that the city knew how to stage a national event and draw hordes of volunteers. Who knew, though, that the community would embrace an eight-day national swim meet — and smash attendance records?

The Omaha Fire Department filled the competition pool as well as a behind-the-scenes warm-up pool. When swimmers broke records, fireworks exploded and flames shot up from poolside. People got to know famous swimmers such as Michael Phelps (right) and saw them walking around the Old Market. If most of us hadn't known the butterfly as well as we knew a fly ball, or appreciated the backstroke like we do a good backfield, at least we recognized great athletes and great performances. Everything went so well that Omaha was awarded the 2012 Swim Trials, too — with the start of the swim competition that year overlapping the end of the CWS. Two major events across the street from each other, both nationally televised. Everything went swimmingly.

OMAHA'S ATTENDANCE OF **160,000** AT THE 2008 TRIALS BEAT THE EVENT'S RECORD BY **50,000**

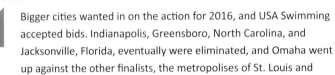

SWIMMING WITH THE BIG FISHES

Bigger cities wanted in on the action for 2016, and USA Swimming accepted bids. Indianapolis, Greensboro, North Carolina, and Jacksonville, Florida, eventually were eliminated, and Omaha went up against the other finalists, the metropolises of St. Louis and San Antonio. When Omaha won, the San Antonio Express-News said a stunned crowd of more than 100 there was shocked. The city's sports chairman said, "It's possible to feel worse, but only post-surgically." A St. Louis headline read, "DUNKED." But an official told the St. Louis Post-Dispatch that the process was fair, especially "when you know what a great job the winning city has done with the event in the past — I've been there both times and knew how high the bar was set."

"We're beating major cities in what we do here."

— Roger Dixon of Omaha, president of the Metropolitan Entertainment and Convention Authority, on securing the bid for the 2016 U.S. Olympic Swim Trials

NCAA BASKETBALL

The CenturyLink Center arena, which has attracted early-round games in the NCAA men's basketball tournament, in 2018 will be home to a regional — the Sweet 16/Elite 8 round, along with bigger cities Atlanta, Los Angeles and Boston. The CenturyLink Center arena, opened in 2003, is home to men's basketball games for the Creighton Bluejays of the Big East Conference. In the 2013-2014 season, in which Doug McDermott (right) was named national player of the year, the Jays drew an average of 17,896 fans, fifth in the nation, behind only powerhouses Syracuse, Kentucky, Louisville and North Carolina, and ahead of Indiana, Ohio State and Kansas.

EACH YEAR THAT OMAHA HAS HOSTED EARLY-ROUND NCAA TOURNAMENT GAMES (1977, 2008, 2012 & 2015), ONE OF THE OMAHA TEAMS MADE IT TO THE TITLE GAME.

WORLD VOLLEYBALL

In 2015, the CenturyLink welcomed an international volleyball competition. The FIVB World Grand Prix, won by the United States, was the first major FIVB event held in America. The arena also has hosted the Final Four of NCAA volleyball.

GOLF

The 2013 U.S. Senior Open golf tournament at the Omaha Country Club generated record revenue and had the second-largest attendance since the tournament began in 1980. "This community knows how to back an event," tournament chairman Patrick Duffy said.

FIGURE SKATING

The U.S. Figure Skating Championships were held at the CenturyLink Center in 2013. The weeklong event drew 90,760.

EQUESTRIAN

In 2017, the arena will host the equestrian World Cup Finals, as selected by the Fédération Equestre Internationale. That followed the success of events for The International, a competition sponsored by the Omaha Equestrian Foundation. Omahans don't have to get dressed up to enjoy dressage, sometimes referred to as "horse ballet," with horses and riders pulling off a series of intricate, technically demanding movements.

OMAHA HOSTED SIX NATIONAL SPORTS EVENTS IN **16 MONTHS** DRAWING MORE THAN **1.1 MILLION** ATTENDEES

"I don't think any city in the country, and maybe in the world, has had a string like that in that time frame."

— Chamber of Commerce President David Brown, after a run of events that created 46 days or nights of national TV coverage from Omaha

BOXING

The CenturyLink in 2014 drew an average of 11,000 to cheer on Omaha's first world champion boxer, Terence "Bud" Crawford, in two title fights. "Anyone who watched the fight on HBO had to have been impressed with Crawford's brilliance in the ring, " boxing writer Kevin Iole wrote after Crawford's victory over Yuriorkis Gamboa, "but the drama of the event increased tenfold because of the loud, boisterous crowd that enthusiastically backed Crawford."

44. *1898 TRANS-MISSISSIPPI EXPOSITION*

OMAHA'S ORIGINAL "BIG EVENT" was like nothing Omaha has seen since. Spawned by the economic downturn known as the Panic of 1893 and inspired by that year's Chicago World's Fair, the Trans-Mississippi & International Exposition showcased the development of the West from the Mississippi River to the Pacific Coast. Among those who pushed for the fair was famed populist William Jennings Bryan of Nebraska, presidential candidate and one-time editor of the Omaha World-Herald. Congress appropriated $100,000, and local businesses raised more money.

GETTING PLASTERED

Photos of the main concourse, with visual reproductions of Grecian and Roman temples, remain amazing to behold. But the structures weren't meant to last. They were made of wood covered with a mixture of hemp fiber, cement and plaster of Paris, and utility workers many years later occasionally would find pieces when digging. Besides the 11 large white buildings, there were dozens of smaller ones surrounding a lagoon in which people took gondola rides. The fair included a miniature railroad, a horse-less-carriage exhibit, exotic dancers from the Middle East, ostriches pulling carriages, a giant seesaw (far right) and much more.

The fairgrounds sat on roughly 200 acres bounded by 16th, 24th, Pratt and Pinkney Streets in north Omaha on land donated by developer Herman Kountze. In the aftermath, part of the land was used for houses, but the center of the fair became Kountze Park.

AMONG THE VISITORS WAS
PRESIDENT WILLIAM MCKINLEY,
WHO SPOKE AT A GOLD-DOMED BUILDING ON OCTOBER 12.
ABOUT 110,000 PEOPLE REPORTEDLY
ATTENDED THE FAIR THAT DAY.
OTHER VISITORS TO THE EXPOSITION INCLUDED APACHE LEADER
GERONIMO AND BUFFALO BILL CODY.

CROWDS
TOTALING
2.6
MILLION
ATTENDED
THE EXPO

STILL STANDING

A gazebo believed to be from Omaha's 1898 "world's fair" sits today in a quiet spot at the city's botanical center, Lauritzen Gardens. The gazebo for decades sat outside the Storz mansion at 37th and Farnam Streets. In recent years, the 10 foot-by-10-foot hexagonal shelter with a metal domed roof was donated to Lauritzen Gardens and restored. Visitors can see it between the Victorian Garden and the Garden of Memories, and imagine an incredible Omaha memory of the late Victorian era.

45. MOVIE PREMIERES

HOO-RAY FOR ... OMAHA? No, it's not Hollywood, but Omaha has been the scene of a few major motion-picture world premieres. Each was a blast, with searchlights, stargazing, limos, crowds, parties and lots of other fun. But the one with the biggest Omaha stamp on it may have been "Boys Town" in 1938, because it not only opened in the Big O but also was shot here. And it had the greatest long-term effect locally because it made Boys Town — originally Father Flanagan's Boys Home — a national household name. That led to decades of fundraising for a place that today is considered a leader in child care research.

The premiere was held in Omaha on September 7, 1938, because Flanagan had made a special request to MGM President Louis B. Mayer to do so. An estimated 30,000 people crowded the streets for the city's first world movie premiere. Fans also lined rooftops and looked out from store windows. The stars had arrived in limousines from the Fontenelle Hotel and mounted a platform to say hello to the huge throng and to listeners over 107 radio stations. Spencer Tracy donated his Academy Award to Boys Town, where visitors can view it in the Hall of History.

STAR POWER

The "Boys Town" premiere attracted stars Maureen O'Sullivan, Spencer Tracy and Mickey Rooney, along with producer John Considine. "This thing makes a Hollywood premiere look like a dying hog," Tracy said at the Omaha Theater on Douglas Street downtown.

"If the picture is great, it is because the great goodness and sweetness and beauty of the soul of this man shines even through me to you."

—Spencer Tracy, motioning to Father Flanagan

30,000 PEOPLE CAME OUT TO CELEBRATE THE "BOYS TOWN" PREMIERE

"UNION PACIFIC"

The April 28, 1939, premiere of "Union Pacific" occurred less than eight months after the "Boys Town" premiere, and Omahans were getting used to the fun and attention. This time about 55,000 turned out for the event. The city staged a four-day celebration called Golden Spike Days, and Omahans dressed and decorated with Western themes.

The premiere took place at the same time at three theaters — the Omaha, the Orpheum and the Paramount — three weeks before the 70th anniversary of the driving of the golden spike that joined the rails of the Union Pacific and Central Pacific in Promontory Summit, Utah. The movie told the story of the building of the transcontinental railroad across the American West.

"THE DESCENDANTS"

In 2011, Omaha director-screenwriter Alexander Payne screened a preview of his movie "The Descendants" at Film Streams in Omaha. Strictly speaking, it wasn't a premiere because it had been shown at film festivals and, five days earlier, in Los Angeles. But Payne always makes sure his hometown get to see his movies as early as possible.

"THE INDIAN RUNNER"

"The Indian Runner," directed by Sean Penn (left, with Dennis Hopper) and filmed in Omaha, Council Bluffs, Ralston, Plattsmouth and surrounding areas, was shown at a sneak preview in Omaha in 1991. It had been shown at film festivals and had a "special premiere showing" the night after Omaha in Los Angeles before opening nationally.

"ON GOLDEN POND"

"On Golden Pond," starring former Omahan Henry Fonda, had a special screening at the Orpheum in Omaha in 1982, two weeks before its national release. The screening benefited the building of a wing at the Omaha Community Playhouse, where Fonda had started his acting career. Technically, it wasn't a world premiere because the film had been shown in Hollywood a few weeks earlier. But the special event was a big deal locally.

HENRY FONDA AND KATHARINE HEPBURN WON
BEST-ACTOR OSCARS

"To have the premiere of the movie here for this cause — it's so right."

— Jane Fonda tearfully told an Omaha crowd

Three Air Force movies drew the attention of Omahans, in part because of the presence of Offutt Air Force Base south of the city.

"STRATEGIC AIR COMMAND"

"Strategic Air Command" opened in 1955 at the Orpheum Theater, part of a two-day celebration of SAC's ninth anniversary. Stars Jimmy Stewart and June Allyson helped cut a three-tiered birthday cake with Gen. Curtis LeMay, and more than 100 newspaper reporters from across the country got briefings about SAC, based at Offutt. The Storz mansion at 37th and Farnam Streets in Omaha was opened to the stars and other dignitaries for opulent parties.

"THE WILD BLUE YONDER"

A parade with 45,000 spectators and three days of events celebrated the premiere of "The Wild Blue Yonder," a WWII drama about "the boys of the Strategic Air Command" who flew the first B-29s. It opened in 1951 at the Orpheum, a week before the national opening.

"A GATHERING OF EAGLES"

"A Gathering of Eagles" was shown at the Center Theater in Omaha in 1963 with stars Rock Hudson and Mary Peach attending. Hudson toured SAC as part of the festivities.

COMMUNITY

In our neighborhoods and suburbs, we occupy a growing place called Omaha. But what makes a community? Not conformity, homogeneity or unanimity, but rather a diversity of ethnicity, religiosity and individuality.

46. BUILDING BLOCKS

OMAHA TODAY SITS IN the midst of a two-state metropolitan area, a long way from its days as "Omaha City" in 1854. The term "Omaha metro area" has come to include a number of smaller cities that still embrace their own identity. And within the city limits are neighborhoods that once stood on their own.

1915: *SOUTH OMAHA*

The city tried to annex the town of South Omaha as early as 1890, when both communities were allowed to vote on the matter, and South Omaha fought it off. South Omaha voters again rejected attempts in 1907 and 1911. South Omahans finally capitulated to the inevitable in 1915 and voted for annexation. Its borders at the time were roughly the Missouri River, F Street, 42nd Street and Harrison Street.

1915: *DUNDEE*

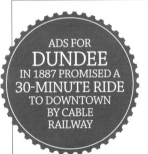

ADS FOR **DUNDEE** IN 1887 PROMISED A **30-MINUTE RIDE** TO DOWNTOWN BY CABLE RAILWAY

The hilltop community, also annexed in 1915, originally was situated between 48th and 52nd Streets and Capitol Avenue and California Street but spread quickly when a streetcar line was extended to reach it. The American Planning Association in 2011 cited the neighborhood for its "varied residential architecture, strong sense of community and ongoing commitment of residents to care for and beautify the neighborhood."

1917: FLORENCE

When Florence was annexed in 1917, it was bounded roughly by the river, Read Street, 40th Street and Florence Heights Boulevard. Florence retains a small-town feel with businesses on 30th Street and a focus on the area's history, which includes the Mormons' stay in the area in the winter of 1846.

THE BANK OF FLORENCE, **CHARTERED IN 1856,** WAS THE **FIRST BANK** IN NEBRASKA

1917: BENSON

Benson, which became part of the city in 1917, was bounded roughly at that time by Blondo Street, 52nd Street, Pratt Street and 72nd Street. It has maintained a community feel with Benson High School and a revived business district that has gained a reputation as a top spot for craft beers.

A 1917 NEBRASKA LAW
ALLOWS THE CITY TO ANNEX
AREAS UNILATERALLY —
YES, WITHOUT ASKING.
THE ONLY LIMITATIONS ARE THAT
THE ANNEXED AREAS MUST BE NEXT
TO THE CITY, UNDER 10,000 PEOPLE
AND INSIDE DOUGLAS COUNTY.
WITH TWO NOTABLE EXCEPTIONS
— THE ANNEXATIONS OF THE TOWNS
OF MILLARD IN 1971 AND ELKHORN
IN 2007 — THE SYSTEM HAS WORKED
WITH LITTLE CONTROVERSY.

A SECRET WEAPON

Nebraska's annexation law has allowed Omaha to benefit from mostly orderly growth while adding to the city's population. The city largely has been able to recapture tax base as the metropolitan area expands, which helps the financial health of the central city. The Des Moines Register once called the ability to annex and grow "Omaha's secret weapon." Unlike cities such as St. Louis and Cincinnati, which still have the same municipal boundaries they had nearly a century ago, Omaha's city limits grow practically every year.

ANOTHER WAY TO GROW

In the late 1940s, the Nebraska Legislature came up with what the recent Des Moines Register article called "an ingenious solution" to the problem of suburban development. The law created a miniature municipality, the inelegantly named sanitary and improvement district. Hundreds of SIDs have levied taxes to pay for streets, sewers, streetlights and other public amenities. Eventually, SIDs are annexed.

1971: MILLARD

Millard was a tiny burg southwest of the city that grew fast after construction of a big Western Electric plant nearby in the late 1950s. As the town's population sped toward 10,000, Omaha leaders said their city's growth to the southwest would be cut off unless the area was annexed. Millard fought bitterly, some residents even hanging an effigy of Omaha's mayor, Gene Leahy. Courts ruled, though, that the state annexation law was constitutional. Millard appealed all the way to the U.S. Supreme Court, which declined to hear the case.

2007: ELKHORN

Four decades after the Millard battle, an annexation conflict played out again with Elkhorn to the west. Its population reached 8,000, and Omaha began steps to annex. This time, the Omaha mayor who drew anger was named (Mike) Fahey, not Leahy. Elkhornites argued that it wasn't simply a case of wanting to keep an identity, but also of wanting to provide their own city services. In a civic drama, Elkhorn itself moved to annex areas that would put the town's population over 10,000 and out of Omaha's legal reach. But the move was made too late, and courts again ruled in favor of Omaha.

KEEPING AN IDENTITY

People still say they live in "Millard" or "Elkhorn" because that is how those parts of Omaha are known. Each still is home to a prominent water tower, emblazoned with the former town's name. And the Millard and Elkhorn school districts, which are independent and separate from cities, continue to thrive under their longtime names.

RALSTON GOES IT ALONE

In the late 1960s, the mayors of Ralston and Omaha shook hands on an agreement that Ralston would not extend its reach any farther than its roughly 1½-square-mile area. In return, Omaha would not make a move for annexation. The deal has held up for nearly 50 years, although annexation talk occasionally resurfaces.

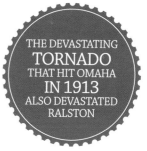

THE DEVASTATING **TORNADO** THAT HIT OMAHA **IN 1913** ALSO DEVASTATED RALSTON

"I love Omaha. I love the north side, and I love the neighborhood I grew up in."

— **Othello Meadows, who leads a nonprofit working to improve north Omaha**

47. NORTH OMAHA

THERE'S MORE TO THE city's northeast area than meets the eye. It is a place of schools, homes, neighborhoods, restaurants, parks and churches, with a sense of community and a diverse population. Long the section of Omaha with the highest poverty, unemployment and crime rates, it also is rich with history and full of plans for improvement. Brigitte McQueen Shew (upper right), founder of the Union for Contemporary Arts, said the many positive traits get overlooked when people "look on us in judgment but never see the wonderful things."

Residents of the Prospect Village neighborhood have actively part-nered with the City of Omaha to improve the area. Neighbors hold festive get-togethers and health fairs, create shared gardens and hold parenting classes and gang-prevention programs.

"North Omaha" encompasses a lot, and often is unfairly painted with a broad brush. The cycle of poverty persists, but many from within the community and from without are trying to improve lives.

LIFELONG RESIDENT AND NEIGHBORHOOD LEADER RONDAE HILL SAID SHE WOULDN'T LIVE ANYWHERE ELSE AND LAUDED "ALL OF THIS POSITIVE MOMENTUM GOING ON."

THE BIRTHPLACE OF MALCOLM X COVERS 12 ACRES OF GREEN SPACE IN THE HEART OF NORTH OMAHA

MALCOLM X BIRTH SITE

The Malcolm X Memorial Foundation visitor center is near 34th and Pinkney Streets, where Malcolm X was born. Rowena Moore created the foundation in 1971 with the goal of keeping alive the legacy of the civil rights leader and his commitment to social justice.

EDUCATION

Nelson Mandela Elementary, a private school with free tuition, opened in 2015. The Lozier Foundation and the William and Ruth Scott Family Foundation funded the conversion of the former Blessed Sacrament Church and School. The building now features a media center addition, with a curved-glass front along North 30th Street, and a new entrance with offices, a cafeteria and commons area in the rear, off Curtis Avenue.

REVITALIZATION

Apartments and town houses are part of an effort receiving backing from investor Warren Buffett and his philanthropist daughter, Susie Buffett. It's called the Highlander 75 North development, the first phase of which includes businesses as well as an educational enrichment complex. The nonprofit Seventy-Five North Revitalization Corp. of Omaha is working on it with Purpose Built Communities, which has turned around neighborhoods in Atlanta and New Orleans, partly by emphasizing early-childhood education and a strong neighborhood school. Howard Kennedy Elementary in Omaha also is part of the effort.

"We want people to realize there's not just this big negative cloud over north Omaha."

— Kyle Keith, president of the North Omaha Neighborhood Alliance

EMPOWERMENT NETWORK

The Empowerment Network, formed in 2006, was honored by the FBI for its efforts to improve circumstances in north Omaha. Willie Barney (left), the group's president, accepted the Director's Community Leadership Award at FBI headquarters in Washington, D.C.

The network also started Omaha 360, a violence prevention initiative that works with residents, religious leaders, police and more than 100 community organizations. An annual event is Harmony in the Park at centrally located Memorial Park, emphasizing the need for all sectors to come together.

After the on-duty death of Officer Kerrie Orozco in 2015, Omaha 360 director Jami Anders-Kemp said the city needed to embrace the togetherness it felt while grieving for Orozco: "In her honor, we need to keep living that out." Barney led prayers in the park, ending with, "Somebody say 'Amen.' Somebody say 'Unity!'"

A GOAL OF METRO, WHICH ALSO HAS CAMPUSES IN SOUTH OMAHA AND ELKHORN, IS TO PROVIDE IMPROVED JOB TRAINING FOR MORE STUDENTS IN THE TECHNOLOGY AND TRADES FIELDS.

METRO COLLEGE

A highlight of north Omaha is the old military post called Fort Omaha, since 1984 home to Metropolitan Community College and since 2009 the site of one of the area's coolest buildings — the $16 million Institute for the Culinary Arts, with seven instructional kitchens, a conference center and, best of all, a chocolate laboratory. The culinary institute will be joined on the south end of campus by a three-building, $90 million project scheduled to open in 2018. It will consist of an academic skills center, the Center for Advanced and Emerging Technology and the Construction Education Center. As with the culinary institute, the project is funded with a combination of public and private money.

48. INWARD GROWTH

THE AKSARBEN VILLAGE AREA IS ESTIMATED TO HAVE AT LEAST **$500 MILLION** IN DEVELOPMENT

AS OMAHA GROWS toward a 1 million metropolitan-area population, not all the expansion occurs outward, away from the core. Development occurs inward, too, notably Aksarben Village and Midtown Crossing. People now flock to both for music, festivals and everyday living. To create a community, it takes a village — not to mention a crossing or two.

AKSARBEN VILLAGE

The 21st century development was built on the former site of the Aksarben horse racing track. Private investment has led to construction of office buildings, apartments, motels, restaurants and a movie theater. The University of Nebraska at Omaha also developed its south campus on the property, including residence halls, its business college and the Peter Kiewit Institute for engineering and technology.

MAMMEL HALL

The University of Nebraska at Omaha adds a college campus feel to Aksarben Village. Mammel Hall, UNO's College of Business Administration building, is one of the buildings north of the retail and restaurant area.

"It's probably one of the hottest areas in town."

— Omaha retailer Mike Sartori

MORE THAN **9,000** ROCKED OUT AT STINSON PARK FOR THE MAHA MUSIC FESTIVAL IN 2015

MIDTOWN CROSSING

An increasingly fun and vibrant place for Omahans to cross paths is the old-town area rechristened as Midtown Crossing. It has resulted in new homes, businesses, restaurants, parking and other investment, as well as outdoor and indoor movies and other public attractions and improvements up and down the street.

Midtown isn't in the middle of the town, but that's the historical name for the area dating back more than a century. The recent development started with the Destination Midtown master plan, created in 2003 by an alliance of corporations, merchants, neighborhood activists and city officials. Mushrooming development took root when two giant employers, Mutual of Omaha and the University of Nebraska Medical Center, began looking at their own backyards.

Ground was broken on Mutual's 15-acre, $365 million Midtown Crossing development in 2007, and it opened in 2010. Five years later, the area was bustling with 850 new residents, 40 businesses, a Westin hotel and vibrant Turner Park. With all that happening in a half-dozen blocks around 33rd and Farnam Streets, other developers began rehabilitating condemned and distressed buildings, attracting millennials with "geeky cool" apartments that include bike lockers, Wi-Fi and other amenities. New apartment buildings have sprung up, too.

THOUSANDS
COME TO
TURNER PARK FOR
JAZZ
ON THE GREEN
EACH SUMMER

"A quiet revolution making transformative change."

— An urban planner, on midtown

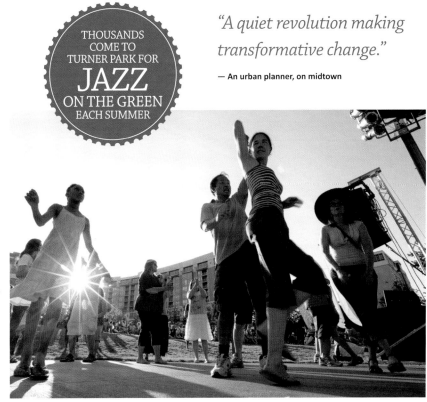

A HIP PLACE TO BE

A once-forlorn commercial district near 40th and Farnam Streets is now dotted with cool restaurants, pubs and shops in an area known as the Blackstone District, for the nearby former Blackstone Hotel. On top of the Mutual of Omaha investment, more than $160 million has flooded into the area.

49. SARPY SUBURBS

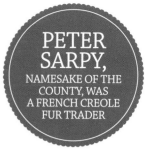

PETER SARPY, NAMESAKE OF THE COUNTY, WAS A FRENCH CREOLE FUR TRADER

A QUICKLY GROWING PART of the metropolitan area is directly south of Omaha, where a trio of Sarpy County towns with French-sounding names — Bellevue, Papillion and La Vista — already combine for nearly 100,000 people.

BELLEVUE

Development around Bellevue has accelerated in recent decades because of the Kennedy Freeway, which connects with Omaha and the Interstate highway system. Bellevue also is the home of Fontenelle Forest, with its miles of hiking trails and views of the river. Bellevue means "beautiful view," so named because of the bluffs overlooking the Missouri River.

MANY AIR FORCE PERSONNEL AND RETIREES LIVE IN THE SARPY COUNTY TOWNS BECAUSE OF THEIR PROXIMITY TO OFFUTT AIR FORCE BASE, WHICH IS ADJACENT TO BELLEVUE.

PAPILLION

Papillion, or "Papio," was named No. 1 by Livability.com among Top Small Towns in America in 2012. It is home to Sumtur Amphitheater, Werner Park baseball stadium and the Omaha Storm Chasers, the Triple-A minor league affiliate of the Kansas City Royals.

PAPILLION GETS HIGH MARKS:

2ND BEST PLACES TO LIVE
— Money magazine, August 2015

4TH VETERAN FRIENDLY CITIES
— Nerdwallet.com, July 2015

9TH HAPPIEST SUBURBS
— Movoto blog, May 2014

MONARCHS

Papillion means "butterfly," the name attached by settlers who marveled at all the butterflies along the creeks, which also are named Papillion. Papillion La Vista High School uses the butterfly in the nickname of its athletic teams, the Monarchs.

LA VISTA

La Vista is the youngest city in Nebraska, incorporated in 1960, and is home to a conference center.

50. COUNCIL BLUFFS

OMAHA AND COUNCIL BLUFFS are hardly twin cities — the former being seven times larger than the latter. Though they are separated only by the Missouri River and can look at each other "up close and personal" when they get up each morning, they haven't always seen eye to eye. The Iowa city adopted casino and greyhound gambling, which led to the demise of the Aksarben racetrack in Omaha. An Omaha mayor once called Iowa "a triple-X-rated state" and charged that the casinos were creating problem gamblers.

Despite the differences, the two towns sit in the same metropolitan area. Tom Hanafan, who served 25 years as mayor of Council Bluffs, quips that his city is part of the largest metropolitan area in Iowa — though most of that metro area is in Nebraska. Long known as a blue-collar town and a railroad center, Council Bluffs in recent times has attracted a high-tech Google data center. In a sense, Omaha and Council Bluffs are separated merely by a hyphen. Said Hanafan: "This amazing region has unlimited opportunities for growth."

TOP 10 GREAT
PUBLIC SPACES
BAYLISS PARK
— American Planning
Association,
October 2014

LOESS HILLS

Only a few locations in the world feature the land formation found on the eastern side of the Omaha-Council Bluffs metropolitan area — the Loess Hills. The defining geographical feature of Council Bluffs was formed 14,000 to 24,000 years ago from glacial silt. Says the Loessfest organization: "These hills nest the city and provide it with immediate access to wildlife, unique natural environments and beautiful views in all directions."

LOESSFEST

Since 2013, Loessfest has attracted thousands to enjoy fireworks, celebrate Council Bluffs and kick off the summer season with music and other events at Tom Hanafan River's Edge Park. Sitting just across the Missouri River from downtown Omaha at the foot of the Bob Kerrey Pedestrian Bridge, the park and the festival have welcomed the Omaha Symphony, the Beach Boys, Chicago and others. The park is an 85-acre preserve and recreational area that includes a Great Lawn and 1,100-seat amphitheater.

PUBLIC ART

Council Bluffs gets extraordinary support, especially from the Iowa West Foundation, for its abstract and sometimes controversial public art. "Every time I come to Council Bluffs," sculptor John Lajba said, "I see this explosion of art. It's all over your city."

CARTER LAKE IS CUT OFF FROM ITS OWN STATE BY THE MISSOURI RIVER

700 LIGHTS ALONG ABBOTT DRIVE SERVE AS THE ENTRANCE TO OMAHA

STRING OF PEARLS

In 1999, an outside consultant said Omaha needed more sparkle. One result, on the road from the airport to downtown, is a beautiful "string of pearls." That bejeweled phrase became the nickname for 700 globe lights along Abbott Drive starting at the airport, through Carter Lake and to downtown. Critics said they caused light pollution, but the bigger problem was hail. Storms in 2011 and 2014 blasted a number of the globes, and the City of Omaha found a more durable replacement. The city also began using LED bulbs, which reduce energy costs. The string of pearls, first completed in 2003, definitely has added sparkle at a time when Omaha made other major improvements along the riverfront. The Peter Kiewit Foundation donated millions to improve the "entrance" to the city, including a distinctive wall, hundreds of trees and the globe lights. After all the civic projects, including the globe lights, the appearance is strikingly different from what was there before. Said Lyn Wallin Ziegenbein, the foundation's executive director emerita: "It was one junkyard after another. It was a very dreary, ugly, decrepit area, and so to change it to this was a stunning change and improvement."

"This project helped to change the way we see our town and built pride in how we know others now see us."

— Lyn Wallin Ziegenbein of the Peter Kiewit Foundation

51. CARTER LAKE

THE CITY OF CARTER LAKE is a curious place north of downtown Omaha that's a geographic oddity — an Iowa town on the Nebraska side of the Missouri River. Carter Lake sat east of the Muddy Mo on the "Iowa side" until 1877, when a flood receded and the river found a new channel. That left an oxbow lake where the river used to flow, and put the town on the west side of the Missouri — the Nebraska side. The lake (called Carter Lake, same as the town) is pretty, and makes a nice welcome today for people who fly into adjacent Eppley Airfield. The odd locale of Carter Lake makes for a confusing state of affairs — actually, for two states.

NEBRASKA — EPPLEY AIRFIELD — CARTER LAKE — Omaha — IOWA

CLUB AND CREIGHTON UNIVERSITY CREWS USE CARTER LAKE FOR ROWING PRACTICE AND COMPETITION

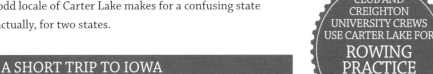

A SHORT TRIP TO IOWA

Some comedian with the Iowa highway department years ago ordered a sign saying "Welcome to Iowa" to be put up along Abbott Drive between Eppley Airfield and downtown Omaha. Huh? If someone just rented a car at the Omaha airport and sees that he's suddenly in Iowa without crossing the river, it must be startling — and confusing, even if it's momentarily and literally correct. Of course, there are no signs less than a minute later saying, "Hope You Enjoyed Your Visit to Iowa." Or, "Welcome Back to Nebraska, We've Missed You the Past Half-Minute."

52. NORTH DOWNTOWN

MAJOR DEVELOPMENTS are reshaping the north downtown area around TD Ameritrade Park. A two-block tract known as "The Yard" is being transformed into a $50 million, three-building campus featuring a hotel, apartments, shops and a Kiewit Corp. international training facility.

Several other projects nearby focus on converting warehouses into apartments as well as commercial and office space.

Omaha architect Michael Alley says incoming residents, visitors and students will feed surrounding restaurants and commercial businesses — "exactly what we were hoping for to create a lively and active neighborhood."

CAPITOL DISTRICT

A 14-story, 333-room Marriott Hotel adds to the developing Capitol District around 10th Street and Capitol Avenue, near the CenturyLink Center. The hotel is the centerpiece of a $205 million project that includes 225 rental apartments, 125,000 square feet of office space, a large parking garage and a central plaza that can play host to large outdoor events.

Tourism leaders say the full-service hotel near the existing Hilton Omaha helps the city compete for conventions. The district is getting a further boost from an adjacent office tower for the HDR architecture and engineering firm.

"After 1854, each new arrival also has in some measure enriched society as a whole. The newcomer, usually with nothing other than his language, religion, physical brawn and a desire to be free, somehow adds a new tint to the social fabric — an indefinable hue that enhances, however slightly, the portrait of the city."

— Harry B. Otis and Donald H. Erickson in their 2000 book, "E Pluribus Omaha: Immigrants All"

53. OMAHA'S MELTING POT

LONG BEFORE ITS BIRTH as a city on the Fourth of July, 1854, Omaha was home to the Omahas — Native Americans who had lived here for 200 years. Chief Big Elk, who died in 1853, had visited Washington, D.C., and returned home to solemnly address the tribe: "I bring to you news which it saddens my heart to think of. There is a coming flood which will soon reach us, and I advise you to prepare for it."

TODAY THE RESERVATION TOWN OF MACY, NEBRASKA, REMAINS HOME TO THE OMAHA TRIBE

The Europeans were coming. As recounted by Harry B. Otis and Donald H. Erickson in their book, "E Pluribus Omaha: Immigrants All," the Omahas signed a treaty and sold their land to the United States, "reserving for themselves a portion on the Missouri River lying some eighty miles north of Bellevue."

The city dates its start at 1854, but the Omahas lived here first. Soon Omaha attracted many from an array of ethnic backgrounds — Irish, Germans, Lithuanians, Greeks, African-Americans, Czechs, Italians, Croats, Serbs, Poles, Swedes, Danes, Mexicans and more. Later came those from Asia, including Vietnamese. In the 21st century, immigrants continue to arrive from Mexico, Latin America, Sudan, Bhutan, Myanmar and elsewhere.

OMAHA PAYS TRIBUTE TO ITS TRIBAL NAMESAKE

At Fort Omaha, an annual Intertribal Powwow "honors the traditional dance, music, artistry and foods of various tribes. ... Dancers in colorful regalia perform throughout the day, including the Gourd Dance that honors military veterans." The University of Nebraska at Omaha, too, hosts an all-nations powwow.

RACIAL MIX

Omaha remains mostly white despite decades of minority growth, with the 2010 Census showing that white residents account for two-thirds of the population.

AFRICAN-AMERICANS AND HISPANICS EACH ACCOUNT FOR ABOUT **12%** OF THE CITY'S POPULATION.

DANES

Omahans might enjoy a Danish for breakfast, but lots of Danes enjoy Omaha all day long. According to U.S. Census data, the Big O is home to more Danish descendants than any other city in the country. Among them are Mogens Bay, Valmont Industries chairman and CEO, who was born in Denmark, and Bruce Lauritzen, chairman of the First National Bank of Omaha and honorary Danish consul for Nebraska. Members of Denmark's Parliament and the Royal Danish Embassy traveled 4,500 miles to Nebraska in 2013 to learn about U.S. business. As the visiting Eva Kjer Hansen explained in Omaha:

"WE WERE LOOKING FOR WHERE IN THE U.S. WAS DOING VERY WELL IN CREATING GROWTH AND JOBS."

SUDANESE

Omaha is said to be home to the largest group of Sudanese refugees in the United States, most of them refugees from civil war in their homeland. Among them:

THE NUMBER OF SUDANESE LIVING IN OMAHA HAS GROWN FROM FEWER THAN 1,200 IN 1998 TO NEARLY 9,000

- Professional model Nykhor Paul, who was discovered by a scout at an Omaha shopping mall when she was 14 and in 2014 joined fellow representatives of the International Rescue Committee to start the ball-drop at Times Square in New York on New Year's Eve.

- Akoy Agau, Nebraska's 2013 player of the year in basketball who started off at the University of Louisville before transferring to Georgetown.

- Deng Ajuet, who appeared in "The Good Lie," a movie about the Lost Boys of Sudan, starring Reese Witherspoon.

A NEIGHBORHOOD EVOLVES

Sudanese youths play basketball at Pulaski Park, which takes its name from a Polish hero of the American Revolutionary War. It is in what once was a Polish immigrant neighborhood of South Omaha.

CROSSOVERS

The Father Flanagan Division of the Ancient Order of Hibernians has held its annual awards banquet at — where else? — the German-American Society Hall. "Lovely place," said a Hibernian. "The Germans really know how to do things." Irish-Americans hope to create an Omaha Irish Cultural Center, just as the American Italian Heritage Society opened a cultural center in 2014 (above).

A POLKA TOWN

German, Polish and Czech cultural groups make sure polka music doesn't stop.

According to census figures for Douglas County residents:

- **26%** are of German ancestry

- **4%** are Polish

- **3%** are Czech

54. WORSHIP

OMAHA LOOKS MUCH like the U.S. in terms of religion. About 49 percent of Omaha adults self-identified as Protestant, similar to the 47 percent nationally. About 24 percent called themselves Catholics, a report said, compared with 21 percent in the U.S. In all, 85 percent in Omaha identified as Christians, compared with 82 percent nationally.

IMPORTANCE OF FAITH

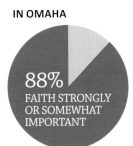

A 2015 survey by the research company Barna Group said religious faith was strongly or somewhat important to 88% of Omaha adults.

IN OMAHA

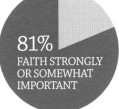

88%
FAITH STRONGLY
OR SOMEWHAT
IMPORTANT

IN THE U.S.

81%
FAITH STRONGLY
OR SOMEWHAT
IMPORTANT

CIVIC INVOLVEMENT

Omaha's Jewish community has made an impact for many years in civic and business leadership. Johnny Rosenblatt and Edward Zorinsky were popular mayors, and Jewish families have operated nationally known businesses such as Omaha Steaks (Simons) and Nebraska Furniture Mart (Blumkins). Borsheims Fine Jewelry was built by the Friedman family, and the old Brandeis department store and the Hinky Dinky grocery stores were owned by Jews. Jesuit-run Creighton University offers the Kripke Center for the Study of Religion and Society and the Klutznick Chair in Jewish Civilization. The University of Nebraska at Omaha runs the Schwalb Center for Israel and Jewish Studies and administers the Fried Holocaust and Genocide Education Fund.

FAST GROWTH

Omaha-area Muslims come from more than 20 countries in the Middle East, Asia, Africa and Europe. According to Lutheran Family Services, which works with refugee families of all faiths, the number of Muslims in the area is roughly double the count from two decades ago. Many have come from Sudan and Somalia. Some Muslims have lived in the area for many years, holding positions in medicine and technology.

MAKING MUSIC

Salem Baptist Church's sanctuary can seat 1,300 on Sundays. Services at Salem Baptist, near 30th and Lake Streets, feature traditional gospel hymns and contemporary music.

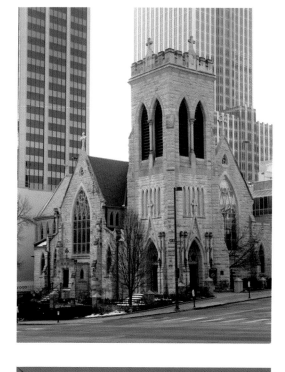

JEWS AND MUSLIMS EACH CLAIM FROM 5,000 TO 6,000 FOLLOWERS IN THE OMAHA AREA

OMAHA'S OLDEST CHURCH

Trinity Episcopal Cathedral is Omaha's oldest church building still in use. Trinity's parish was organized in 1856, two years after Omaha's founding, and the congregation relocated to its present site in 1867.

OMAHA'S CATHEDRAL

Construction of St. Cecilia Cathedral, the centerpiece of the Omaha Archdiocese, began in 1905. It first was used in 1916 but not fully completed until bells were hung in its twin towers in 1959.

A PLACE TO BE AT EASTER

King of Kings Lutheran draws more than 5,000 worshippers to its Easter service at the CenturyLink Center. The church had used the Aksarben Coliseum and the Civic Auditorium as attendance grew. In 2008, King of Kings moved into the CenturyLink to accommodate the worshipers. More than 200 volunteers served as greeters at the entrances and along hallways in 2015.

55. TRI-FAITH CAMPUS

"The Tri-Faith Initiative is the embodiment of basic Midwestern and biblical values —
of having neighbors, getting to know your neighbors and treating your neighbors with respect."

— Bob Freeman, board chairman of the Tri-Faith Initiative

A ONE-OF-A-KIND PLACE

Elsewhere, such disparate houses of worship happen to sit in close proximity, and in some other places the faiths may gather under one roof. But leaders of the Omaha effort say they know of no other place in the world that intentionally has set out to build such separate faith structures on the same site.

THE IRONICALLY NAMED Hell Creek runs through a sloping, 35-acre landscape where Omaha is building a unique tri-faith campus for a synagogue, a church and a mosque. A spokesman for the coordinating Tri-Faith Initiative called the project "unparalleled in history."

It is not a merger of faiths, and proselytizing will be forbidden. "This is not about finding the lowest common denominator," said the Rev. Eric Elnes of Countryside Community Church, "but rather the highest common denominator."

THE $60 MILLION PROJECT IS FUNDED WITH DONATIONS

On 9/11, Rabbi Aryeh Azriel (above) and members of the Temple Israel congregation helped stand guard at an Omaha mosque. That made an impression, and two months later 300 people of Jewish, Muslim and Christian faiths met in friendship. Conversations continued in ensuing years.

In 2009, about 1,100 met for a stirring "Dinner in Abraham's Tent: Conversations in Peace." All three faiths descend from the biblical Abraham, and the evening ended with "salaam, peace and shalom." Land eventually was purchased at the former Highland Country Club south of 132nd and Pacific Streets, where Temple Israel built its synagogue, which opened in 2013. In 2015, Countryside Church announced plans to build on the campus, and the American Muslim Institute of Omaha broke ground for a mosque.

"Welcome to a place built by dreamers," local Muslim leader Dr. Syed Mohiuddin said at the groundbreaking. Added Dalia Mogahed of Washington, D.C., former executive director of the Gallup Center for Muslim Studies: "This project captures the best of America. Appropriately, it is in the heart of the country, Omaha."

Plans call for a fourth interfaith building on the campus and a span over Hell Creek — to be called Heaven's Bridge.

FULL FAITH

Proselytizing will be prohibited at the Omaha campus, but that doesn't mean that each faith cannot live its religion in the fullest sense. For example, a church can display a cross and the synagogue a Star of David.

The Rev. Eric Elnes (above), senior minister of Countryside Church, said his flock walks "fully in the path of Jesus without denying the legitimacy of other paths that God may create for humanity."

WHY OMAHA?

Why would people in Omaha, of all places, set out to build a synagogue, a church and a mosque at the same location? "Omaha is the right place. Omaha is THE place. It is welcoming," said Dr. Syed Mohiuddin (above), a local Muslim leader. "You don't hear about any kind of problems with different faiths in Omaha. That is part of our character."

56. MORE TO COME

CIVIC VISIONARIES OF Heartland 2050 expect Omaha's population to reach 1.3 million by the mid-21st century. The city is expected to grow by more than 100,000 to about 550,000, and Council Bluffs is projected to add about 20,000 to 80,000. The 2050 project, sponsored by the Metropolitan Area Planning Agency, predicts rapid growth in the Sarpy County suburbs — Bellevue to 85,000, Gretna to 62,000 and Papillion to 60,000.

Growing especially fast is Gretna, which had a 2010 population of 4,441 but was estimated at 5,584 in 2013. It includes a number of households with one spouse working in Omaha and the other in Lincoln.

METROPOLITAN OMAHA IS EXPECTED TO ACHIEVE THE 1 MILLION-POPULATION MILESTONE BY 2023.

FUEL FOR RAPID GROWTH IN GRETNA

The Nebraska Crossing Outlets mall in Gretna opened in November 2013 and saw about 4 million shopper visits in its first year.

FESTIVE US

Omaha is a party town, where people use any ol' excuse to gather and celebrate. Parades, fireworks, music, dancing, food, fundraising — you name it. Festive is our middle name, and festivals are our game. We deal with serious stuff, too, but know the value of letting off steam with a theme. Just turn the calendar, and there's something to celebrate.

57. STARTING WITH A BANG

THOUSANDS GATHER AROUND the million little lights in the trees of Gene Leahy Mall downtown on New Year's Eve to ring in the new year. Fireworks light the sky as choreographed music plays, horns honk and people cheer. It's noisy, but tamer than Times Square in New York — with a family-friendly Omaha time. Not midnight, but 7 p.m. Earlier, at noon, Durham Museum and the Henry Doorly Zoo celebrate, too, with lots of events for kids. Oh, and lest auld acquaintance be forgot, adults later gather with friends across the area to raise a cup of kindness yet and sing "Auld Lang Syne."

OMAHA SHOOTS OFF FIREWORKS AT THE **FAMILY-FRIENDLY HOUR OF 7 P.M.**

58. FUNKY FEBRUARY

OMAHA'S WACKIEST, TACKIEST most irreverent celebration pokes fun at the high-society Aksarben Coronation. More than 1,000 people attend the quirky Groundhog Prom, an "alternative costume ball" on or near Groundhog Day, wearing outrageous outfits spoofing celebrities, politicians or other headline-makers. A woman once came as the famous nude painting at the Joslyn, "Return of Spring," wearing a body suit and carrying a big wooden frame. As one attendee put it: "There's this whole underground scene with interesting people in this city — people willing to purchase body glitter and wear it all night."

THIS GROUNDHOG WON'T RUN AWAY

Fontenelle Ferd, the weather-forecasting groundhog at Fontenelle Forest, issues a local outlook every February 2. Ferd, unlike the more famous Punxsutawney Phil, is stuffed and spends the rest of the year in a display case.

The Omaha Film Festival screened 16 narrative features, seven full-length documentaries and 74 short films over six days in 2015.

The festival, which began in 2006, features new films that have not reached distribution deals. Local filmmakers, such as Bellevue's Matt Gengel (below), are among those who submit their work.

Among big names appearing in the festival's narrative films in 2015 were Simon Pegg, Jason Alexander, Dennis Farina, Peter Stormare, Malcolm McDowell, Jane Seymour, Keith Carradine, Bruce Greenwood, Dee Wallace and James Caan.

But short films by Nebraska filmmakers, or shot in Nebraska, also are audience favorites at the festival held in March.

59. A TOAST TO O'MAHA

THE FATHER FLANAGAN DIVISION of the Ancient Order of Hibernians stages a St. Paddy's Day parade downtown on a Saturday close to St. Patrick's Day. A horse colored green (temporarily) pulls a carriage honoring the grand marshal, and crowds gather to cheer clever floats, bagpipers, bands and other marchers. With spring around the corner, people joyously sing and hoist a Guinness on St. Paddy's Day to celebrate the end of winter.

60. OUTDOOR EGGSTASY

SPIRITS PICK UP AS THE landscape greens up. Easter egg hunts draw big crowds — nearly 3,000 kids at Bellevue Christian Church, 2,000 at Spring Lake Park, 1,000 at Skinner Magnet Center, among others in March and April. April's rain kisses us, and we brighten at the prospect of warmer months even as we keep an eye out for storms, twisty or otherwise.

PAPILLION HID 22,000 EGGS FOR ITS 2015 HUNT

TREE PLANTING

Arbor Day originated in Nebraska, and the suburban Omaha town of Papillion annually holds a big celebration of trees, with a 2015 theme of "Safe in the Shade."

THE GROUP GREEN BELLEVUE GOES BIG ON EARTH DAY, WITH A RECYCLING THEME, "LIGHTEN THE LOAD"

APRIL IS PUBLIC HEALTH MONTH, AND THE GREATER OMAHA YMCA URGES KIDS TO GET OUT AND EXERCISE, HOSTING A HEALTHY KIDS DAY.

61. OH MI, OH MAYO

FOR MORE THAN THREE DECADES, CINCO DE MAYO HAS MEANT A BIG PARADE DOWN SOUTH 24TH STREET, THE OLD SOUTH OMAHA BUSINESS DISTRICT.

WHAT'S THE MONTH of May without Cinco de Mayo? The celebration marks the day in 1862 when underdog Mexican forces defeated the more numerous French invaders at the Battle of Puebla, but most gringos aren't aware of that. An elderly Irish-American woman in Omaha thought it was nice that new neighbors of Mexican descent were staging a parade in honor of the Irish, confusing County Mayo with Cinco de Mayo. Just as everyone is Irish on St. Patrick's Day and all Americans celebrate the Fourth of July, everybody can join the fun on the Fifth of May. Mariachi music, dancers, floats and horseback riders as well as Mexican pottery and dresses, not to mention tacos, tortas and chili lime mangos on sticks — what's not to like?

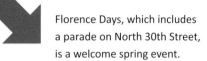

FLORENCE DAYS

Florence Days, which includes a parade on North 30th Street, is a welcome spring event. The Florentine Players present a melodrama as part of the festivities. As a male character remarked to his love interest, "You're the purdiest gal I've seen all winter. 'Course you're the only gal I've seen all winter."

62. AMORE AND ART

SANTA LUCIA FESTIVAL

Many Omahans of Italian descent trace their ancestry to the town of Carlentini, Sicily, which has venerated the martyred St. Lucy since 1621. Grazia Bonafede Caniglia immigrated to the United States in 1900, and in 1925 she founded the Santa Lucia Festival to give immigrants in Omaha a strong connection with their former country and to deepen their faith in their new home. The tradition remains, with a procession carrying a statue of St. Lucy from St. Frances Cabrini Church in the Little Italy neighborhood to the modern riverfront at Lewis & Clark Landing. A festival there fills the air with music and with the aroma of cooked peppers, sausage, marinara sauce and other Italian food. For everyone, that's amore. Some still tear up at a tenor's singing of a soulful, heartfelt "Saaan-taa, Lu-cheee-ee-ah!"

THE FESTIVAL WAS FOUNDED IN **1925** BY GRAZIA BONAFEDE CANIGLIA FOR ITALIAN IMMIGRANTS

"What's interesting to me is how Omaha has changed and has kind of a global view of what goes into making a dynamic city."

— Vic Gutman, organizer of the Summer Arts Festival for all of its 41 years

SUMMER ARTS FESTIVAL

The three-day Summer Arts Festival each June attracts artisans from across America who set up booths and sell their wares. The festival attracts local crowds, too, and has done so for more than four decades.

It was organized in 1974 by 23-year-old newcomer Vic Gutman. He stayed, still runs the festival and receives about 400 applications a year from people who want one of the 135 booth spaces. In 2008, straight-line winds described as "a hurricane on the Plains" destroyed about a third of the booths. But artisans had made it to cover, and no one was hurt.

Gutman, who encountered resistance to his festival idea when he arrived in Omaha, says attitudes are far different now. "The city embraces young people and their creative energies. There are young professionals groups and business incubators. And corporations understand the importance of keeping young talent in Omaha and nurturing it."

63. LIGHTING UP THE SKIES

OMAHANS LOVE FIREWORKS. Not just watching professional fireworks shows, ooh-ing and ahh-ing. No, we like to shoot 'em off, too. Firecrackers, fountains, parachutes, sparklers, snakes … . In Douglas and Sarpy Counties, 100 fireworks stands do big business — in the millions — selling various fireworky things, including those annoying whistling projectiles. Nonprofit groups are issued permits and get a cut of the revenue, which funds such things as scholarships, mission trips and equipment for youth sports teams. The City of Omaha began allowing stands in 2011, increasing competition for suburban fireworks dealers that once had a monopoly on fireworks sales. For the Fourth of July and New Year's Eve, the Omaha ordinance allows the use of any fireworks that are permitted by state law. Crowds still like to gather for big shows like The World-Herald's at TD Ameritrade Park and Bank of the West's at Memorial Park. But the colorful, ear-popping nights around the Fourth, especially, leave a smoky haze over neighborhoods across the city.

THE CITY OF OMAHA BEGAN **ALLOWING FIREWORKS** STANDS IN **2011**

THE WORLD-HERALD'S FIREWORKS SHOW BEGAN IN 1985 AT ROSENBLATT STADIUM. THE SHOW NOW GOES OFF AFTER THE COLLEGE HOME RUN DERBY AT TD AMERITRADE PARK. THE VIEW IS SPECTACULAR, EVEN FROM ACROSS THE MISSOURI RIVER IN COUNCIL BLUFFS.

MEMORIAL PARK FIREWORKS AND CONCERT

In addition to fireworks, Omahans love music and the outdoors, and that's a perfect summer combination to fill normally quiet Memorial Park. Huge crowds have gathered on the park's slopes to hear nationally known bands and singers and to watch the skies sparkle and glow.

The event was started in 1987 by Commercial Federal Savings and Loan to mark its 100th birthday. A spokesman said he hoped several thousand would hear the Tommy Dorsey Orchestra and The Lettermen, but attendance was 20,000.

Crowds quickly grew, the event later was taken over by Bank of the West, and in 2015 organizers estimated 75,000 came to hear Joan Jett, a member of the Rock and Roll Hall of Fame. For the first time, the overflow caused some folks to sit on blankets on the south side of Dodge Street, Omaha's main east-west thoroughfare.

64. SUMMER IS LOOKING UP

IN THE WARMTH of summer, eyes often lift skyward for events like the Nebraska Balloon & Wine Festival and the Offutt air show. At the festival, lighted hot-air balloons launch up, up and away, and 18 wineries provide mellow drinks. Some of the balloons are even more colorful than the one in "The Wizard of Oz" that says "State Fair Omaha." The festival, south of 204th and Q Streets, includes pony rides and other fun for kids. The Defenders of Freedom Open House and Air Show at Offutt Air Force Base attracts precision flying by Navy Blue Angels and Air Force Thunderbirds, and lots of other airplanes, such as those in World War II-style dogfights.

THE AIR SHOW IS A REMINDER THAT OFFUTT'S ANNUAL ECONOMIC CONTRIBUTION TO OMAHA IS HUGE — ROUGHLY $1.35 BILLION

NATIVE OMAHAN DAYS

Omahans, and those with Omaha ties, make their way back to the city for this celebration in north Omaha. The event is a time of celebration, reunion and reminiscence, of seeing old friends and reconnecting. The sponsoring Native Omahans Club provides scholarships and promotes "cultural, social and recreational activities for the inner-city and north Omaha community." The 2015 event featured a parade, an arts festival and live music.

65. A FEST OF SEPTEMBER

SUMMER'S END LONG has been marked not by the equinox, but by Labor Day. Omaha celebrates the holiday weekend with Septemberfest, a "Salute to Labor." With fewer jobs today in the building trades and manufacturing and more in the service sector, not nearly as many people in Omaha belong to labor unions. But organized labor's societal contributions aren't forgotten. Labor leaders say Americans take for granted some gains that resulted in large part from unions, such as weekends off, the 40-hour workweek, health care and Social Security. Terry Moore, longtime president of the Omaha Federation of Labor, said in 2015: "My concern is American jobs, U.S. jobs. I have a simple mission in life. Can a couple with three children buy a house, a car and send the kids to college?" For Moore and others, all the hard work in putting on Septemberfest is a labor of love.

SEPTEMBERFEST INCLUDES A **75-ENTRY PARADE** AND A MULTI-DAY **RIVERFRONT FESTIVAL**

SWEET PARADE

Can't wait for Halloween? Septemberfest parade participants traditionally toss candy along the route, and some children bring bags to help collect the goodies.

66. FALLING FOR AUTUMN

AS TREES TURN, many start thinking about Halloween costumes. But others start picking out other kinds of duds — for the jeans-wearing crowds at the Aksarben Stock Show & Rodeo and then the evening-gown-and-tux attire of the Aksarben Coronation & Scholarship Ball. Both events are produced by the forward-thinking philanthropic group that since the 1890s has spelled Nebraska backward. Formerly called River City Roundup, the rodeo and stock show at the riverfront CenturyLink Center includes a downtown parade, but with lots of horses and tractors. There's also a pancake feed, a barbecue contest, a 4-H livestock show, the rodeo and a concert.

THE GLITTERY HARVEST-TIME CORONATION, HONORING FAMILIES FOR CIVIC CONTRIBUTIONS, CULMINATES IN THE CROWNING OF A KING AND QUEEN OF THE MYTHICAL KINGDOM OF QUIVIRA.

67. HOLIDAY LIGHTS FESTIVAL

THANKSGIVING DAY IN OMAHA means more than turkey, dressing, families and giving thanks.

That night, the mayor flips on the holiday lights at Gene Leahy Mall. A free public concert follows at the adjacent Holland Performing Arts Center. As part of the Holiday Lights Festival, lights also shine on 24th Street — in South Omaha between L and Q Streets, and in north Omaha around 24th and Lake. The holiday lights shine throughout the season, until extinguished a few days into the new year.

AT 6 P.M. ON THANKSGIVING THE MILLION OR SO TINY LIGHTS FLIP ON IN THE TREES LINING THE GENE LEAHY MALL DOWNTOWN

GIVING BACK TO OTHERS

As part of the festival, Omahans contribute to the "Shine the Light on Hunger" campaign, providing more than a million meals through the Food Bank for the Heartland. The lighted ConAgra Foods Ice Rink on the company's downtown campus charges $5 admissions that are donated to the food bank. ConAgra then matches them.

68. CHRISTMAS AT THE DURHAM

THE CHRISTMAS TREE AT THE DURHAM IS USUALLY A BLUE SPRUCE, **MORE THAN 40 FEET TALL**

SPRUCING UP THE HOLIDAYS each December is a festival starting with the lighting of a festooned evergreen tree. The tradition in the Great Hall of the Durham Museum, the former Union Station, dates to the station's earliest days in the 1930s, when Union Pacific decorated and displayed large trees for travelers. The station closed in 1971, but was saved from demolition a few years later through the efforts of a dedicated group of volunteers. "Christmas at Union Station" includes entertainers, choirs, school musicians, a bubble-wrap stomp for kids and an ethnic holiday festival. The more, the merrier.

ENTERPRISE

With Fortune 500 companies and others with a global reach, as well as a top national ranking for tech workers, Omaha welcomes competition with bigger cities. Nonprofits play a big role, too, and the Big O ranks high in philanthropy.

BERKSHIRE RANKS 4TH IN THE FORTUNE 500, ONE SPOT AHEAD OF APPLE

THE WORLD LOVES FAMED INVESTOR Warren Buffett for his ethics, humor and folksy ways, and Omahans appreciate him because he never turned away from his home and his office in Omaha — a city where he says you can think more clearly than in New York. Speaking of the Big Apple, Yankee slugger Alex Rodriguez called Buffett the business equivalent of Babe Ruth. "What's been most impressive about Warren," A-Rod said of his pal, "is how humble he is and how he's just been able to keep his Omaha way about him."

Buffett lives and works on Farnam Street, not on Wall Street, and remains our town's greatest ambassador. Buffett lives in the house he bought in 1958, with next-door and across-the-street neighbors like everyone else. He has long extolled his hometown's "clean air, low crime rate, good schools and Midwestern work ethic." Eitan Wertheimer, chairman of Iscar Metalworking Cos. in Israel, said on CNBC that he tried to get Buffett to visit Iscar before he paid $4 billion for 80 percent of the company. "He told me he loves to sleep in his bed in Omaha," Wertheimer said. "That's his most desirable place for spending time."

OPEN INVITATION

Each spring Buffett welcomes his Berkshire Hathaway shareholders to Omaha — 40,000 in 2015 — and he enjoys receiving letters about how well Omahans treated them. He also welcomes college classes to Omaha throughout the year for one-day sessions. He quipped to more than 100 from Harvard: "Now you can say you've been to Omaha. That's a real status symbol."

He has taken time to teach ukulele at the Girls Inc. social services agency. And when a driver accidentally rear-ended his car on a rainy day, he told her it was OK — and sent her flowers and See's chocolates. The woman, who was ticketed, was on her way to meet friends for dinner at an upscale restaurant. Buffett — this is so Warren — continued down Leavenworth Street to pick up burgers at Bronco's.

THE OMAHA WAY

It's nice to think Buffett embodies the Omaha way, but what is that exactly? Modesty and self-reliance? A feeling that we don't need to live on the coasts to be high achievers and enjoy a high quality of life? A quiet sophistication without putting on airs? Often referred to as the Oracle of Omaha, he made his bed in Omaha and is happy to sleep in it. He has a modest way about him, and maybe that's the simplest way to describe the Omaha way.

Warren Buffett is invested in Omaha. Berkshire Hathaway employs thousands at its companies based here:

- Applied Underwriters
- BH Media Group
- Borsheims
- Central States Indemnity
- Homestate Insurance
- MidAmerican Energy
- National Indemnity
- Nebraska Furniture Mart
- Northern Natural Gas
- Oriental Trading
- Real estate sales and services

Thousands of other Omahans work for Berkshire companies that do business in Omaha, including:

- BNSF Railway
- Helzberg Diamonds
- Dairy Queen

A FASCINATION WITH NEWSPAPERS

Buffett, whose parents worked on the Daily Nebraskan at the University of Nebraska, is a longtime fan of newspapers. In fact, he delivered papers as a boy. In 2011, Berkshire Hathaway purchased the Omaha World-Herald, which created BH Media Group. The Berkshire division, headquartered in Omaha, now owns more than 70 newspapers and other media outlets in 11 states. Buffett explained his reasons for investing in a struggling industry at the time of The World-Herald purchase: "I'm most comfortable, actually, with a real, honest-to-God newspaper in my hand," he said, and added, "I think a newspaper can contribute to that well-being that the community enjoys over time."

ORIENTAL TRADING CO.

Born in Japan, Harry Watanabe bought an Omaha gift shop in 1932 that became the Oriental Trading Co. Today it is part of Buffett's Berkshire Hathaway, which purchased it in 2012 for $500 million. Not bad for a knickknack company that sells novelties and gifts as well as party, craft and school supplies. Oriental Trading employs about 2,000 during peak seasons under the slogan "Making the World More Fun."

In the 1950s, Oriental Trading became a major supplier to carnivals, and in the 1970s it expanded by sending out millions of catalogs. By the 1990s, it was growing through the Internet. The company recently has acquired MindWare, which makes "brainy toys for kids of all ages," and SmileMakers, which caters to the dental and health care markets.

Oriental Trading donates regularly to charity. One of its most unusual gifts was the 2010 shipment of 10,000 boxes of crayons to Haiti to be used in therapeutic drawings by children, many of them orphaned by the earthquake.

ORIENTAL TRADING PROVIDES **MORE THAN 40,000** PRODUCTS

AT THE 2015 BERKSHIRE SHAREHOLDERS MEETING IN OMAHA, ATTENDED BY ABOUT 40,000, ORIENTAL TRADING SOLD **$5 RUBBER DUCKS DEPICTING BUFFETT AND HIS VICE CHAIRMAN, CHARLIE MUNGER.** IN HONOR OF BERKSHIRE'S 50TH ANNIVERSARY, EACH WAS SHOWN IN A BUSINESS SUIT.

NEBRASKA FURNITURE MART

A tiny Russian immigrant founded an Omaha furniture store that became America's largest and now has sunk roots deep in the heart of Texas. As the Dallas Morning News put it: "Who inspired a company to come to the cockiest state in the nation, build a braggadocio store the size of nine football fields — in the land of Friday Night Lights, no less — and then give another state's name top billing?" That would be the late Rose Blumkin, the legendary "Mrs. B," who stood 4-foot-10 but thought big — very big. And now her Nebraska Furniture Mart, run by her descendants, gives the Cornhusker State bragging rights in the state that boasts, "Everything is bigger in Texas."

After a 1975 tornado struck her Omaha store on 72nd Street, she rebuilt bigger and better. She contributed greatly to the community, and her name graces the Rose Blumkin Jewish Home and "The Rose," the Rose Blumkin Performing Arts Center. The Mart, with a huge array of appliances, electronics and other home furnishings, expanded to Kansas City, Kansas, in 2003, and to The Colony, Texas, outside Dallas, in 2015. The Texas store is larger than three Walmart Supercenters.

MRS. B

Rose Gorelick was born outside Minsk, Russia, and followed husband Isadore Blumkin to America in 1917. In the basement of his downtown clothing shop in 1937, she started selling furniture with the slogan "sell cheap and tell the truth." Truth to tell, she did sell cheap, with small margins – and it worked. Mrs. B never really retired, buzzing around on a motorized cart and working nearly to the end of her life in 1998, when she died at 104. The company jokes that 104 is now its mandatory retirement age.

WARREN BUFFETT EXPECTS

$1 BILLION

IN ANNUAL SALES FROM THE NEW TEXAS STORE

BUFFETT COMPLETED THE DEAL FOR NEBRASKA FURNITURE MART WITHOUT AN AUDIT AFTER OWNER ROSE BLUMKIN GAVE HIM A PRICE. "IF SHE RAN A POPCORN STAND, I'D WANT TO BE IN BUSINESS WITH HER," BUFFETT SAID.

The corporate giants headquartered in the Big O are all homegrown: Berkshire Hathaway, Union Pacific, Kiewit Corp. and Mutual of Omaha. It's a healthy number for a city Omaha's size. A University of Cincinnati study found a direct correlation between the number of Fortune 500s and the quality of a city's cultural, medical and educational organizations, as well as the availability of sports and leisure activities. Such corporations are active in their communities, contributing dollars to local causes and workers to serve on civic and charitable boards.

		36th St.
★ KIEWIT ★ BERKSHIRE HATHAWAY		35th St.
		34th St.
MUTUAL OF OMAHA ★		33rd St.
		31st St.
Farnam St. Douglas St. Dodge St.		24th St.
UNION PACIFIC ★		
		14th St.

CLOSE PROXIMITY

Many Fortune 500 companies are headquartered in nearby suburbs of major cities, but Omaha's sit within a healthy walking distance of each other. Union Pacific is at 14th and Douglas Streets downtown, and the three others sit less than two miles to the west, practically shoulder to shoulder. Mutual of Omaha is at 33rd and Dodge, with Kiewit and Berkshire Hathaway based in the Kiewit Plaza tower at 36th and Farnam.

70. KIEWIT CORPORATION

THE KIEWIT CORP. of Omaha built more miles of the Interstate highway system than any other contractor — so many that Fortune magazine dubbed then-CEO Peter Kiewit "the Colossus of Roads." But the company has helped build America in many other ways, too. A construction, mining and engineering company that's one of the largest contractors in the world, Kiewit tackles big projects.

The company was founded in Omaha in 1884 by Peter Kiewit, a bricklayer of Dutch descent. He had three sons, one also named Peter Kiewit, who led Peter Kiewit Sons' Inc., from 1924 until his death in 1979. The company expanded greatly while building military installations during World War II and the Cold War.

Kiewit, which ranks high in Best Places to Work voting, is one of the largest employee-owned companies in the world. One of the few construction companies big enough to take on billion-dollar projects, it remains a business colossus.

KIEWIT IS ONE OF THE **LARGEST EMPLOYEE-OWNED COMPANIES** IN THE WORLD

GLOBAL (AND LOCAL) REACH

Across the United States, Canada and Australia, Kiewit projects include transportation, water and wastewater, power, oil, natural gas and chemicals. The firm has built bridges, buildings, dams, tunnels and much more, including the world's largest glazed geodesic dome (below) at the Henry Doorly Zoo & Aquarium in Omaha.

PETER KIEWIT

Peter Kiewit was active in civic affairs, and in 1962 purchased the Omaha World-Herald to keep it locally owned, rather than run by a national chain. The newspaper eventually became employee-owned — except for 20 percent owned by the charitable Peter Kiewit Foundation — until purchased in 2011 by Warren Buffett.

71. UNION PACIFIC

THE UNION PACIFIC LAID ITS first rail in Omaha near the Missouri River on July 10, 1865, on the way to linking the nation east and west. Ever since, the railroad and the city have shared a lasting marriage — a parallel course, like two iron rails of a track to forever. And today the U.P., whose catchy commercial jingles once dubbed it "The Great Big Rollin' Railroad," has thrived as an old-economy business in a high-tech world. A 19th century startup has become a 21st century stalwart.

A freight-carrying behemoth, Union Pacific directs more than 9,000 locomotives, 32,000 route miles and 47,000 employees in 23 states, ranging from Chicago and New Orleans to California. Omaha investor Warren Buffett, whose office sits two miles from U.P. headquarters, in 2009 bought the Burlington Northern Santa Fe. BNSF and U.P. are far and away the dominant carriers in the western U.S.

The Union Pacific mark on Omaha is indelible. Motorists driving west on Interstate 80 cross into Nebraska and see two old U.P. locomotives perched prominently on a hilltop at Lauritzen Gardens, the city's botanical center. The U.P. Museum, including relics from the Lincoln funeral train, is housed in a former Carnegie public library in Council Bluffs. And the heart of modern-day Omaha activity — the CenturyLink Center arena and convention center and TD Ameritrade Park — sits on the former U.P. repair-shop property, with railroad memorabilia displayed outside (below).

THE 25-STORY, GLASS-EXTERIOR DOWNTOWN HEADQUARTERS OPENED IN 2004

LINCOLN AND UNION PACIFIC

Honest, Abe Lincoln had so much to do with its start that the U.P. calls him its founding father. He had visited Council Bluffs across the river before his presidency and foresaw the general area as the eastern terminus of a transcontinental railroad. As president, he signed the Pacific Railway Act of 1862, and the unprecedented project moved ahead from Omaha and Sacramento, much later recounted by Stephen Ambrose in his book "Nothing Like It in the World." A largely Irish immigrant U.P. workforce laid mile after mile of rail across the Plains and through difficult landscape, meeting up with the largely Chinese crews of the Central Pacific at Promontory, Utah, on May 10, 1869. The historic final linkage was hammered together with a golden spike.

FOR YEARS MUTUAL HAS SPONSORED ATHLETES, SUCH AS PRO GOLFERS WHO WEAR MUTUAL OF OMAHA CAPS. THE COMPANY HAS ASSISTED WITH THE 2008, 2012 AND THE COMING 2016 U.S. OLYMPIC SWIM TRIALS. A BANNER 60 FT. WIDE AND 245 FT. HIGH SHOWING A SWIMMER IN MIDSTROKE ONCE GRACED MUTUAL'S FACADE.

72. *MUTUAL OF OMAHA*

INSURANCE IS A BIG industry in Omaha, with about 30 corporate headquarters. But the firm most associated with the city is the one that has carried the civic name around the world — Mutual of Omaha.

MUTUAL OF OMAHA WAS ORIGINALLY NAMED MUTUAL BENEFIT HEALTH AND ACCIDENT ASSOCIATION

Simpler often is better. And so a company founded in 1909 with the cumbersome name Mutual Benefit Health and Accident Association eventually took its more straightforward, iconic name. The then-chairman, V.J. Skutt, had started calling it Mutual of Omaha in the 1940s, so the formal change in 1962 was a natural.

In Omaha, the company often is referred to simply as "Mutual," and the area around it, west of downtown, as "the Mutual neighborhood." The company is such a symbol for the city that when a CBS News documentary during the Cold War dramatized the effect of a nuclear attack on Omaha, it depicted Mutual's Indian-brave logo on the 14-story headquarters building being blown to bits.

Mutual in recent years built the Midtown Crossing development just east of the main offices at 33rd and Dodge Streets, with condos, apartments, a hotel, a parking structure, restaurants and shops. A sloping greensward there, connected to Turner Park, has attracted crowds of 6,000 or more for free summertime Jazz on the Green concerts.

Executives and employees have contributed to many civic boards and good causes. For more than a century, the company has been good for the city, and vice versa. You might say the feeling is mutual.

EVERYONE KNEW THE NAME

Americans got to know the company in the 1960s with the weekly TV show, "Mutual of Omaha's Wild Kingdom." Mutual told host Marlin Perkins (left) to show lots of action. Once, when a 10-foot anaconda tried to coil itself around Jim Fowler (above), Perkins' rugged assistant, Marlin had to jump into a muddy South American river to help. Fowler often appeared on "The Tonight Show With Johnny Carson," and when an animal nipped Johnny, Big Jim quipped: "That's no problem, we have Mutual of Omaha insurance."

73. BUILDERS

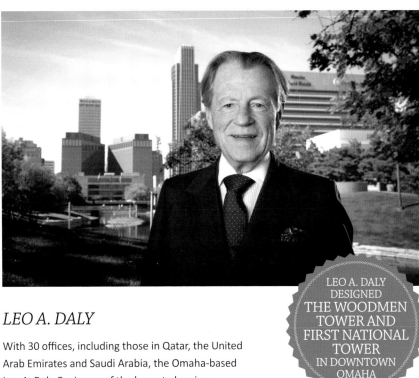

LEO A. DALY

With 30 offices, including those in Qatar, the United Arab Emirates and Saudi Arabia, the Omaha-based Leo A. Daly Co. is one of the largest planning, architectural, engineering and interior design firms in the world. From its headquarters at 8600 Indian Hills Drive, Daly oversees a wide range of projects in all 50 states and more than 87 countries.

In 2015, the firm celebrated the 100th anniversary of its founding in Omaha by Leo A. Daly, whose son, Leo A. Daly Jr., took it international. He also was an Omaha civic leader, and in the 1960s persuaded Woodmen of the World that downtown needed a signature structure, which became the 30-story Woodmen Tower — at the time, the tallest building between Chicago and Denver. The Daly firm designed it, and three decades later designed the 45-story First National Tower. Daly also has designed most of the Boys Town campus.

The company's nearly 800 design and engineering professionals have completed a wide range of projects, including an airport expansion in Berlin and a 30-story air traffic control tower at John F. Kennedy International Airport in New York City, as well as designs relating to transportation, health care, hotels, water supply, the military and more. Of America's top 333 architectural and engineering firms, Building Design + Construction magazine rated Leo A. Daly Co. 14th.

The chairman and CEO is Leo A. Daly III (above), whose next-door neighbors in Washington, D.C., in 2001 were a couple who had just moved from a white house — the former president and first lady, Bill and Hillary Clinton.

LEO A. DALY DESIGNED **THE WOODMEN TOWER AND FIRST NATIONAL TOWER** IN DOWNTOWN OMAHA

ROSEMARY DALY

Rosemary Daly, wife of Leo A. Daly Jr., served on the Daly board of directors and was an Omaha force in her own right. She often purchased art for the company's projects and was known as a gracious hostess and volunteer. A Creighton University business graduate and the sister of Omaha native Jackie Gaughan, longtime Las Vegas developer and casino owner, she died in 2015 at age 96.

HDR

The Omaha-based global architectural and engineering firm is the ninth-largest U.S. design firm, according to Engineering News-Record. With about 900 staffers in Omaha, the employee-owned company's impact on urban landscapes and skylines is huge. In 2015, it made another big impact, this time with plans to build a downtown office building of 18 to 20 stories in its hometown. Founded in 1917, HDR approaches its centennial with an expanding workforce and will move from its headquarters near 84th and Dodge Streets to the new building at 12th Street and Capitol Avenue at the start of 2019.

Long known by its former name of Henningson, Durham and Richardson Inc., HDR has designed many hospitals and has worked on such projects as the Tappan Zee Bridge replacement in New York, the Hoover Dam bypass, the San Antonio River Walk and the Cleveland Clinic Abu Dhabi in the United Arab Emirates.

HDR HAS **10,000** EMPLOYEES IN 225 LOCATIONS AROUND THE WORLD

CHUCK DURHAM

Civil engineer Charles "Chuck" Durham married his college sweetheart from Iowa State, Margre, and in 1940 joined the Omaha firm of her father, the Henningson Engineering Co. It later became Henningson, Durham and Richardson Inc. and then HDR. In his time there, it grew from 15 employees to 1,700.

Durham, who died at 90 in 2008, attributed his success to luck and titled his autobiography "Lucky."

Lucky Chuck lived a high-achieving life and did much for Omaha, which was lucky that he lived in the Big O.

THE FIRM'S PROJECTS HAVE INCLUDED
THE HOLLAND PERFORMING ARTS CENTER, AKSARBEN VILLAGE AND TD AMERITRADE PARK.

Omaha has an "unmatched quality of life."

— **CEO George Little**, on moving HDR's headquarters to downtown Omaha

74. FORTUNE 1,000 COMPANIES

THE OMAHA AREA ALSO is fortunate that five companies from the Fortune 1,000 are headquartered here. They are Green Plains, TD Ameritrade, Valmont Industries, West Corp. and Werner Enterprises.

TD AMERITRADE

Along with Charles Schwab, said TD Ameritrade CEO Fred Tomczyk, Joe Ricketts pioneered the American online brokerage industry. "He brought Wall Street to Main Street and helped average Americans take control of their financial future."

Ricketts launched a company in 1975 after deregulation allowed brokers to set their own commissions. By 1997, his company charged $8 per online trade, and Ricketts embarked on a $20 million advertising campaign.

His American Holding Corp. became TD Ameritrade after a merger with TD Waterhouse. TD traces to Toronto Dominion Bank, a major shareholder. Ricketts and his family remain the largest shareholders, though he retired in 2011 to concentrate on entrepreneurship and philanthropy. Forbes magazine estimated his net worth then at $2.3 billion, but he appeared in a humorous Omaha Press Club Show skit, "Who Wants to Be a Jillionaire?"

PUTTING DOWN ROOTS

Omahans feared that TD Ameritrade might leave the city, but the company solidified its roots by building a 12-story headquarters and a four-building campus in the Old Mill area of west Omaha. And the company became the name sponsor of downtown Omaha's 25,000-seat stadium, TD Ameritrade Park, the home of the College World Series.

HOMAGE TO PAST

The glass on the outside of TD Ameritrade's headquarters appears to be randomly dotted with clear rectangular windows, but the pattern on the 12-story structure is intentional. Architects, at TD Ameritrade's request, arranged the clear panes of windows so that the outside walls resemble strips of old-fashioned ticker tape.

JOE RICKETTS AND THE RICKETTS FAMILY

Ricketts has become a household name, and not just in Omaha. Pete Ricketts (right) of Omaha serves as the 40th governor of Nebraska, and brother Tom Ricketts (second from left) is the CEO of the Chicago Cubs, owned by the Ricketts family. But it all started with dad Joe Ricketts (center), a national online brokerage pioneer who founded what became TD Ameritrade. Laura (left) and Todd (second from right) live in Chicago.

WEST CORP.

In 1986, West was founded by Mary West to handle telemarketing calls, and she was joined a year later by husband Gary West. The company in 2015 sold its call-center unit and is moving to higher technology businesses, such as providing emergency alerts to school parents and staff, advice to employees enrolled in workplace benefit plans and software that supports the nation's 911 emergency telephone system.

The Wests sold most of their stake in West Corp. in 2006 and "retired" to San Diego. But they forged a new life in Southern California as major philanthropists and owners of Thoroughbred race horses, several of which have run in the Kentucky Derby.

GREEN PLAINS

Green Plains is an ethanol producer that has grown quickly on the strength of selling ethanol, corn oil and cattle feed that is a leftover from distilling corn into fuel.

GREEN PLAINS REVENUE HAS MORE THAN DOUBLED SINCE 2009, TO MORE THAN **$3 BILLION** IN 2015

WERNER ENTERPRISES

One of the most remarkable business stories from the Omaha area started out as one man and a truck – Werner Enterprises, one of the nation's five largest trucking companies.

Founder C.L. Werner was honored in Washington, D.C., in 2012 as a Horatio Alger Distinguished American. The Big Blues are everywhere, including in the nation's capital. A Werner truck is part of a permanent exhibit of vehicles at the Smithsonian Institution.

CLARENCE "C.L." WERNER

In 1956, when Clarence was 19, he borrowed a few hundred dollars to buy his first truck. He grew it into a $2 billion international business whose semitrailers, known as "Big Blues," are seen on highways coast to coast.

WERNER PLAYS BALL

Werner Enterprises bought the naming rights to Werner Park, home to the Storm Chasers, Omaha's minor league baseball team. The stadium can seat more than 8,000 people for baseball games and features a statue of baseball Hall of Famer Bob Gibson, an Omaha native. Clarence "C.L." Werner and Warren Buffett were among the initial local figures to fund the project. Sitting atop the stadium's scoreboard is a 42-foot-wide-by-14-foot-high Werner Park sign that is roughly the size of a Werner Enterprises semitrailer truck.

VALMONT INDUSTRIES

Valmont makes mechanized irrigation equipment and industrial systems. Valmont and another Omaha-based company, Lindsay Corp., together account for about 75 percent of total U.S. irrigation sales. CEO Mogens Bay says that Valmont, by the nature of its business, makes the world a better place. "We have an obligation to help feed the world," he said. "It's not just about selling pipes and pumps." That's only part of Valmont's business, however. The company also is a major manufacturer of poles and other steel structures for lighting, traffic control, wireless communication and power utilities markets. Valmont has operations in 23 countries and offers 27 brands from more than 90 manufacturing facilities.

THE BIGGEST COMPANY YOU'VE NEVER HEARD OF

If some thought Omaha-based AGP never would amount to a hill of beans, well, they didn't know beans. It is the largest cooperative soybean processing company in the world. A vice president says that with annual revenues of more than $5 billion, low-profile AGP is "the biggest company you've never heard of."

AGP'S ANNUAL REVENUES TOTAL MORE THAN $5 BILLION

The farmer-owned co-op, long known as Ag Processing Inc., would flirt with the Fortune 500 list, if it met all the criteria.

AGP, with about 1,100 employees, began in 1943 and expanded greatly in 1983. It is "a co-op of co-ops," representing more than 170 cooperatives and 250,000 farmers in the U.S. and Canada. The company processes and markets U.S. agricultural products around the globe.

75. FAMILIAR BRANDS

THIS IS THE BEEF STATE

Omaha long has been known as a place to enjoy succulent restaurants steaks, which is appropriate in the Beef State. Though an urban area on the "east coast" of a 450-mile-wide state, Omaha benefits from Nebraska's status as an agricultural titan.

In the 1950s, the South Omaha Stockyards stood as the largest meatpacking center in the United States, with cattle-laden delivery trucks often stacked for miles on L Street. But the industry de-centralized, and by the '70s the "Big Four" packers — Armour, Cudahy, Swift and Wilson — had shuttered their plants.

Nebraska has cattle grazing on 24 million acres of rangeland and pasture and is blessed with underground water sources. The state, with 1.9 million people, feeds and markets more than 5 million head of cattle per year — nearly a fifth of the 26 million in the U.S.

BEEF IS NEBRASKA'S LARGEST INDUSTRY, WITH AN ANNUAL IMPACT SAID TO EXCEED $12 BILLION

OMAHA STEAKS

Think of Omaha, and lots of people across the country think of steaks, in large part because of a homegrown company called — what else? — Omaha Steaks.

The company doesn't disclose the names of its clientele, but actress Katharine Hepburn let it be known before her death at 96 that she was a weekly customer. Omaha Steaks often makes the news. When a man's home lost power in St. Petersburg, Florida, neighbors ran cords to his house, a newspaper reported, "so his recent order of Omaha Steaks wouldn't spoil." A few years ago, a customer in the Catskill Mountains of New York called to say her order wasn't on her doorstep. A duplicate order was sent from Omaha, but the original order — what was left of it — soon was found in the woods, the shipping box showing bear claw and teeth marks.

In the fifth generation of ownership by the Simon family, Omaha Steaks is a great supporter of the arts and other Omaha charities. Said Todd Simon, senior vice president: "We owe everything to Omaha, really. Including our name."

SAY IT SIMPLY

The company didn't always go by such a short, snappy name describing where it is from and what it sells. Founded in 1917 as the Table Supply Meat Co., it promoted "Omaha steaks" for years before adopting that name in 1966. Today it is the most recognizable brand of beef in America and the leading direct marketer of steaks and other frozen gourmet foods.

RFD-TV

Omaha-based RFD-TV purchased taxidermied figures of TV cowboy Roy Rogers' faithful horse and dog — Trigger and Bullet — and has shown them around the country, including in a nationally televised Rose Parade from Pasadena, California, on New Year's Day. They are based in Omaha.

Patrick Gottsch, who grew up in Elkhorn watching Roy Rogers and other shows of the era, attempted to start RFD-TV in 1988. He relaunched it in 2000 as a nonprofit corporation before transitioning to for-profit in 2007. It shows rodeos, cattle auctions and ag market reports, as well other shows such as reruns of "Hee Haw," "The Mary Tyler Moore Show" and "WKRP in Cincinnati."

Gottsch, who has moved some operations of his Rural Media Group to Nashville, Tennessee, plans on more growth. One of his board members, former U.S. Secretary of Agriculture Clayton Yeutter, praised his persistence and success. "It's just the kind of entrepreneurial success story that you see almost uniquely in the United States," said Yeutter, a Nebraska native who met Gottsch in Washington, D.C., in 2008. "I had no idea who he was, and this guy walks in looking like a hippie. And it turned out he was a Cornhusker."

THE COWBOY WAY

"I get why Roy saved Trigger and Bullet in the first place, I get it," Gottsch (above) said of the stuffed horse and dog. "He saved them to keep the memories alive that 'The Roy Rogers Show' and movies and living the cowboy way and what the Western lifestyle represents."

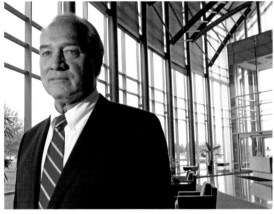

GALLUP

On Omaha's riverfront sits Gallup University, a campus without a student union, fraternities or sororities, let alone a football team. But the folks at old "Gallup U." definitely stress a team approach — attracting executives and managers from client companies far and wide and training them to build on their employees' strengths.

GALLUP COLLECTS DATA IN MORE THAN 160 COUNTRIES

Wait a minute. Gallup? As in the world-famous Gallup Poll? Yes, it's one and the same. Though the polling is handled elsewhere, the Omaha riverfront campus is a key part of the Gallup Organization, which studies human nature and behavior. With world headquarters in Washington, D.C., Gallup designs management systems, publishes books and offers management courses.

George Gallup established the Gallup Poll in New Jersey in the 1930s. Gallup prides itself on being "the world's greatest question-asker" and on "discovering truth and maximizing performance." It doesn't fill a stadium or stage homecoming parades, but Gallup University gives lots of folks an education in Omaha.

THE CLIFTON FAMILY

In 1969, psychologist Donald Clifton co-founded Selection Research Inc. in Lincoln, Nebraska. SRI bought Gallup in 1988 and took the Gallup name. In 2000, Donald's son, then-CEO Jim Clifton (above), quietly met with Omaha Mayor Hal Daub, explaining that Gallup was thinking of moving from Lincoln. Gallup liked that Omaha voters had approved building a riverfront convention center and arena, and in 2003 the company opened its campus practically next door, about a five-minute drive from Eppley Airfield. Gallup and the Clifton family foundation in 2015 announced a $30 million donation to the University of Nebraska-Lincoln to establish the Don Clifton Strengths Institute to help train new leaders.

WOODMEN OF THE WORLD

The iconic Woodmen Tower of late has been seen in a different light — or lights. The white-exterior building, illuminated for years with bright, white light, now often is bathed in various softer hues. Blue for Creighton basketball and autism, red and black for UNO hockey, red and green at Christmas, pink for breast cancer awareness, orange and blue for World Cancer Day. Also, red for International Red Cross Day and green for St. Patrick's Day, Earth Day, Arbor Day and the Girl Scouts' birthday. For patriotic days, what else? Red, white and blue. The computer-controlled LED bulbs that project the light last longer than previous technology and use one-third of the energy.

The late Ed Zorinsky, an Omaha mayor and U.S. senator, quipped that people flying into town could wonder if they were arriving in the city of WOODMEN. That's because the word, in capital letters, is on all four sides at the top of the tower. Joseph Cullen Root, the founder, is said to have coined the Woodmen name from a speech he heard about woodmen clearing forests to provide shelter for their families — and from his desire for the Woodmen to protect its members from financial disaster. A fraternal organization, Woodmen operates in all 50 states and counts more than 700,000 members.

PEREGRINE FALCONS

Peregrine falcons for thousands of years lived mostly on cliff tops, far from predators — and from human eyes. As the birds became endangered, conservationists who feared that they might be wiped out realized that a tall building could serve the same function as a cliff top. And so they placed nesting boxes on buildings, including on a ledge outside the 28th floor of the Woodmen Tower.

Peregrine couples mated, and the population rebounded. Since the birds were introduced at the Woodmen in 1988, more than 75 falcon chicks have been hatched there.

People watch on the Internet as baby falcons take their first flaps and try to survive. It's been called true reality TV because three out of four falcons don't make it past their first year, dying from illness, accidents or violence. Sometimes feathers fly. A state wildlife official calls falcons "nature's fighter jets." In 2015, a male from the top of the State Capitol in Lincoln zoomed to Omaha and battled a male at the Woodmen Tower to a stalemate before returning home.

(badge) THE WOODMEN TOWER IS OMAHA'S **SECOND TALLEST** BUILDING

SIGNING THE FINAL BEAM

Opened in 1969, the tower is home to the Woodmen of the World Life Insurance Society, founded in Omaha in 1890. (A previous 19-story structure, built in 1912 and called the WOW Building, stood at 14th and Farnam Streets and was razed by implosion in 1977.) The 30-story Woodmen Tower is the second-tallest building in Omaha, trailing only the 45-story First National Tower.

IN OMAHA DIRECTOR ALEXANDER PAYNE'S 2002 MOVIE, "ABOUT SCHMIDT," JACK NICHOLSON PLAYED WARREN SCHMIDT, A RETIRING ACTUARY FOR WOODMEN.

76. CONAGRA

CONAGRA MAKES FRENCH FRIES FOR MCDONALD'S

THE REMOVAL OF OLD WAREHOUSES KNOWN AS **JOBBERS CANYON** CAUSED CONTROVERSY AMONG PRESERVATIONISTS. IT BECAME THE SITE OF THE CONAGRA CAMPUS.

FOLKS WALKING NEAR THE popular Old Market shopping and restaurant district downtown often have come across the smiling visage of an iconic American — Chef Boyardee. Well, it's actually a bronzed figure of the famed chef, which has greeted visitors in an outdoor plaza on the campus of food giant ConAgra.

The Fortune 500 company announced in 2015 that it would move its headquarters to the Chicago area. The bronzed chef still was smiling, but the decision produced sadness locally because several hundred jobs will be relocated and others will be eliminated. The company, though, will maintain a significant presence in the Omaha area.

Founded in 1919 as Nebraska Consolidated Mills, the company changed its name to ConAgra — a combination of consolidated and agriculture — in 1971. Then-CEO Charles "Mike" Harper rejuvenated the operation, partly by acquiring others companies such as Banquet Foods and Nabisco, and ConAgra thrived.

In 1988, it considered moving its headquarters to another city, but ended up staying, which became a turning point for Omaha. The city still was smarting from the departure of Enron (formerly Northern Natural Gas Co.) to Houston, a move led by the infamous CEO Ken Lay, who eventually drove the company into the ground. Knoxville, Tennessee, had made overtures to ConAgra to move its headquarters. The Nebraska Legislature responded by enacting tax incentives and exemptions, and Omaha leaders assembled property for the ConAgra campus, another important part of riverfront development. The Heartland of America Park, with a lake and fountain, was built beside ConAgra, and other major developments followed.

CHEF BOYARDEE

ConAgra's Chef Boyardee sculpture is not a cartoon figure or a corporate creation — it is based on a real person, chef Hector Boiardi, a hotel chef and restaurateur before he opened a packaged Italian foods company as Chef Boy-Ar-Dee in the 1920s. Boiardi died in 1985 at 87, and ConAgra Foods acquired the company in 2000.

The sculptor was John Lajba of Omaha, who also created The Road to Omaha, which symbolizes the College World Series and sits at the entrance of TD Ameritrade Park. Lajba, who had viewed many photos of Boiardi, explained at the 2011 unveiling, in which the sculpture was revealed by peeling away a very large "can" of the chef's famed pasta: "He was a man who had a lot of class and a lot of charm. I really want it to feel like his whole demeanor is that he's relaxed, he's at home, and he's eager to meet the citizens of Omaha."

OTHER CONAGRA LABELS

There's more than just Beefaroni. Some of the company's other top brands:

- Healthy Choice frozen foods
- Marie Callender frozen foods
- Orville Redenbacher popcorn
- Reddi-wip dessert topping
- Slim Jim snacks

77. BEDROCK COMPANIES

OMAHA TAKES PRIDE as an incubator of early-21st century businesses and for being named the top city for tech workers. But the startups and other moderns stand on a bedrock of roughly 150 surviving companies and organizations that started in the rough-and-tumble Omaha of the late 19th century.

FIRST NATIONAL

First National Bank of Omaha is a subsidiary of First National of Nebraska, the largest privately owned banking company in America. Most shares of the company that traces its history to 1857 are controlled by the Lauritzen family, with Bruce Lauritzen serving as chairman.
First National — its name since the 1860s — is the oldest national bank west of the Missouri River. It has branches in seven states and is the nation's fifth-largest agricultural lender.

THE TOWER

In the 1990s, the bank had considered building in the suburbs but decided to stay downtown. It built a 45-story office tower, as well as a technology center and a child care facility. The tower is Omaha's tallest building.

FIRST NATIONAL IS HOME TO THE ANNUAL VERTICAL CHALLENGE RACE "TREK UP THE TOWER." HUNDREDS COMPETE TO CLIMB 40 FLOORS, 870 STEPS, AND 633 FEET INTO THE SKY.

RENZE DISPLAY

Renze Display was founded in 1895 by Gus Renze, who purchased floats from that year's Mardi Gras parade in New Orleans and shipped them to Omaha. They were refashioned for "electric night parades" and for the Knights of Aksarben Coronation & Ball. Renze advertising signs now welcome millions of passengers each year at Eppley Airfield.

NP DODGE

Other longtime companies also succeed through generations of families, such as NP Dodge, "America's oldest family-owned, full-service real estate company." It was founded in 1855, the year after Omaha began, by Nathan Phillips Dodge, brother of Grenville Dodge, who became a Civil War general and a founder of the Union Pacific Railroad. The first N.P. Dodge was succeeded by his son of the same name, and then by former World War II pilot N.P. "Phil" Dodge and N.P. "Sandy" Dodge. In 2014, N.P. Dodge V, known as Nate Dodge, became the company president.

Omaha's longtime families sometimes intertwine. Nate Dodge's wife, Meg, is a daughter of First National Chairman Bruce Lauritzen and his late wife, Kimball. Nate's lifelong best friend is Bishop Scott Barker, head of the Episcopal Diocese of Nebraska. He is descended from the Rev. Joseph Barker, an early Omahan whose published "Barker letters" colorfully describe the city's beginnings.

J.P. COOKE CO.

The J.P. Cooke Co., founded in 1887 by James Cooke, still is filling orders from across the nation for badges, tags and time stamps. It operates in the Old Market, run by brothers Warren and John Cooke, with a youthful influx of the next generation belying the notion that too many Cookes spoil the broth.

78. FRANCHISING

MCDONALD'S POPULARIZED AMERICAN franchising, but Omaha has produced several such companies. It's big business. The University of Nebraska at Omaha's College of Business Administration includes the Center for Innovation, Entrepreneurship & Franchising, and the University of Nebraska-Lincoln hosts the International Center for Franchise Studies.

HOME INSTEAD

One of America's most successful franchising companies started on a dining-room table in Omaha. At his mother's home in the Cathedral neighborhood, Paul Hogan (right) created Home Instead Senior Care, starting with $18,000 in savings. He and his wife and co-founder, Lori, in two decades have expanded it into a $1 billion annual business. Home Instead is the world's leading provider of nonmedical, in-home care for seniors. The company provides clients, typically 77 to 83, with companionship and nonmedical help such as meal preparation and housekeeping. The ingenious idea behind the company was that seniors, rather than moving in with relatives or to assisted living, would much prefer to stay home instead.

HOME INSTEAD HAS MORE THAN 1,000 FRANCHISES IN 50 STATES AND 18 COUNTRIES, INCLUDING CHINA

GODFATHER'S PIZZA

Willy Theisen knocked a hole in the wall between his bar and an adjacent restaurant near 99th and Q Streets and began selling pizzas, launching Godfather's in 1973 and selling it a decade later for $306 million.

OTHER OMAHA FRANCHISES:

- Little King
- Merry Maids
- The Maids
- Right at Home In-Home Care and Assistance
- National Property Inspections Inc.

"Omaha is a boomtown," said a 2014 article on Bloombergview.com by writer and Nebraska native Tim Siedell.

"The greater Omaha area, which will soon surpass 1 million people, now boasts one of America's top neighborhoods (Dundee, according to the American Planning Association) as well as one of the top places to live (Papillion, according to CNN Money). Not to mention arguably more ... billionaires and millionaires per capita than wherever you are this very minute. That includes you, New Yorkers."

NO. 1 FOR PAID INTERNSHIPS

Omaha earned another national distinction, especially for young folks looking for a place to start a career — the No. 1 city in the U.S. for paid internships.

INTERNMATCH'S 2015 STATE OF COLLEGE HIRING REPORT SAID MORE THAN 80% OF INTERNSHIPS IN OMAHA ARE PAID, AN AVERAGE OF $12.28 PER HOUR. THE PERCENTAGE RANKS WELL AHEAD OF SECOND-PLACE SAN JOSE, AT 74%.

"Omaha has a pretty diversified economy," an InternMatch spokesman said, "and two of its biggest industries are utilities and manufacturing, which are among the top three industries that pay interns."

79. PHILANTHROPY

OMAHA'S ECONOMIC SUCCESS hasn't just lined people's pockets or fattened their bankrolls. If you ask "What gives?" in the city these days, the answer might not be "what" but "who." Just about everyone gives — and in varying degrees their donations have produced vibrant public-use structures and benefited countless nonprofit organizations.

SUSIE A. BUFFETT

Sometimes called "Susie Junior," Omaha philanthropist Susan A. Buffett has made a big impact of her own through her Sherwood Foundation. The only daughter of investor Warren Buffett and his late wife, Susan T. Buffett, Susie has donated millions.

Robin Hood rode through Sherwood Forest, according to legend, robbing from the rich to give to the poor. The Sherwood Foundation doesn't rob anyone, but it's surely an example of the rich helping the poor. The foundation has donated millions to Omaha Public Schools. It also advocates for early-childhood education and is hoping to lessen the frequency of unwed teen pregnancies.

She serves on the national board of the social service agency Girls Inc., and has helped bring big names to Omaha to raise funds for the local Girls Inc. Among them have been then-U.S. Sen. Barack Obama, first lady Michelle Obama, Archbishop Desmond Tutu, former Secretary of State Madeleine Albright, tennis great Billie Jean King and three Clintons: Bill, Hillary and Chelsea.

BENEFITING FROM BERKSHIRE WEALTH

Estimates are that over the years, longtime investors with Omaha-based Berkshire Hathaway Inc. have given and pledged well more than $1 billion. That includes donations that may be at least partially routed through the Omaha Community Foundation and coordinated by Heritage Services. Many Omahans who have invested through the decades donate in their hometown. The Holland Performing Arts Center is one high-profile example of projects funded in part by major donations tied to Berkshire wealth. Others:

- Mammel Hall at the University of Nebraska at Omaha, funded largely by Carl and Joyce Mammel.
- Othmer Hall at the University of Nebraska-Lincoln, funded by Donald and Mildred Topp Othmer.
- The Stanley and Dorothy Truhlsen Lecture Hall at the Durham Museum.
- The Truhlsen Eye Institute at the University of Nebraska Medical Center.
- The Ruth and Bill Scott Student Plaza at the NU Med Center. The plaza is surrounded by buildings the Scotts helped fund.
- Seemann Stadium at Central High School (above), supported by Lee and Willa Seemann.
- The Olson Center for Women's Health at the NU Med Center, supported by Dorothy and Leland Olson.
- The Fred & Pamela Buffett Cancer Center at the NU Med Center, supported by Warren's cousin Fred and Fred's wife.

OMAHA COMMUNITY FOUNDATION

Philanthropy's importance to Omahans is evidenced by the Omaha Community Foundation's 2014 ranking of No. 5 among the nation's community foundations for the amount given away. The foundation handles charitable giving for more than 1,300 individuals and families. More than $1 billion has been granted to Omaha-area nonprofits since the foundation was created in 1982. It is the nation's 17th-largest community foundation. It's not just the wealthy who donate. Since 2013, the foundation has sponsored "Omaha Gives." The annual 24-hour event promotes donations to nonprofits. In 2015, nearly $9 million was raised in more than 47,000 donations to 704 organizations. Separate from the community foundation, thousands of Omahans take part in charity galas and fundraisers for good causes throughout the year.

"It's phenomenal right now to be in Omaha. When I'm asked by peer foundations what our secret is, I joke that it's like retail: location, location, location."

— Sara Boyd, president and CEO of Omaha Community Foundation

WALTER SCOTT JR.

The chairman emeritus of Peter Kiewit Sons' Inc. not only has donated untold millions personally but also has encouraged others to give to a variety of projects, including those that help young people. His donations have contributed to many other Omaha construction projects that benefited the city, but also have improved education. Scott helped found the Building Bright Futures Foundation, aimed at improving academic performance, increasing high school graduation rates and getting more Omaha-area students into college. He also was the person most responsible for creation of the Peter Kiewit Institute on the grounds of the old Aksarben racetrack. The institute combines the resources of the University of Nebraska at Omaha's College of Information Science and Technology with the University of Nebraska-Lincoln's College of Engineering, and makes "real world" connections between education and industry. He also has funded numerous scholarships and donated to construction of UNO residence halls known as Scott Village and has contributed to many other Omaha causes.

HERITAGE SERVICES

Heritage Services, co-founded by Walter Scott Jr. (below), has raised nearly a half-billion dollars for public-use buildings that have transformed the city. Through the organization, major donors insist that operators of new buildings have the resources and ability to sustain significant, broadly appealing programs far into the future. Among the projects on which donors have collaborated for the betterment of Omaha:

- Holland Performing Arts Center
- Orpheum Theater renovation
- Joslyn Art Museum
- Durham Museum
- CenturyLink Center
- TD Ameritrade Park
- Strategic Air Command & Aerospace Museum
- UNO's Baxter Arena
- Lauritzen Gardens Conservatory

"Walter builds beyond brick and mortar. He builds people."

— John Gottschalk, retired World-Herald publisher, on Walter Scott Jr.

PENGUINS KNOW WHOM TO THANK

Scott and his late wife, Suzanne, years ago were talking with Dr. Lee Simmons of the Henry Doorly Zoo about the variety of fish that could be displayed by building an aquarium at the zoo. Then she asked, "Couldn't we have penguins also?" Simmons recalled: "That's how we ended up with what is unquestionably the best penguin exhibit in North America and perhaps even the world."

The Suzanne and Walter Scott Aquarium opened in 1995 with penguins and much more. The Scotts once flew two baby gorillas to the Omaha zoo in their private plane. Those are just examples of the many ways the acclaimed zoo grew with help from the Scotts.

The Pioneer Courage Park sculptures are 25 percent larger than actual size. Bruce Lauritzen's great-grandfather, Tom Davis, was one of the pioneers who helped to found Omaha in 1854. Optimism, courage, determination and confidence were the qualities Lauritzen said he hoped the sculpture gardens would portray.

THE SCULPTURES ARE PART OF A **$300 MILLION** COMMITMENT TO DOWNTOWN FROM FIRST NATIONAL BANK

THE ARTWORK IS ONE OF THE **LARGEST** EXTENDED DISPLAYS OF BRONZE SCULPTURE IN THE WORLD

LAURITZENS AND FIRST NATIONAL BANK

The Lauritzen family, associated with First National Bank, has provided major support for Lauritzen Gardens and commissioned the artwork in Pioneer Courage Park. Larger-than-life sculptures of pioneers, bison and geese wend their way through blocks of the downtown Omaha business district, an homage to the settlers who built Omaha and the landscape and wildlife they encountered. Pioneer Courage Park, depicting a wagon train leaving Omaha and proceeding along a dry creek bed, sits on the north side of Capitol Avenue between 14th and 15th Streets. The Spirit of Nebraska's Wilderness Park at the southeast corner of 16th and Dodge Streets features bronze and stainless steel sculptures of 58 Canada geese over a fountain plaza, representing the American flight from the industrial age to the information age. In between those two is the park link, five bison traversing sidewalks, public planters and buildings before stampeding. One bison even goes through the corner of a building.

"What I like about the story of the great wagon train migration across America is the daring, the tenacity and the inventiveness of the pioneer spirit that opened the West."

— Bruce Lauritzen, chairman of First National Bank of Omaha and the great-grandson of Tom Davis, who helped settle Omaha in the 1850s

DURHAMS' LEGACY

Charles (right) and Margre Durham, associated with architectural and engineering giant HDR, helped fund a number of noteworthy projects. The Durham Museum is Omaha's history museum in the beautifully renovated former Union Station. The Durham Research Center and Durham Research Plaza are major parts of the University of Nebraska Medical Center, where a robot is named "Chuck" in Durham's honor.

At the University of Nebraska at Omaha, students learn at the Durham Science Center and the Charles W. Durham School of Architectural Engineering and Construction. Iowa State also has recognized Durham, with the naming of the Durham Great Hall at the Memorial Union.

80. PAYING THE BILLS

WHEN YOU SWIPE your credit card at a store anywhere in the developed world, chances are that the payment's electronic path goes through Omaha.

First Data, the Fortune 500 payment-processing giant, employs 5,000 in Omaha, where it was born in 1971. Though its headquarters left the Big O in 1992 and today are in Atlanta, Omaha remains the principal base of operations for the company's financial services division.

First Data CEO Frank Bisignano said in 2015 that Omaha is the company's "backbone" and its "heart and soul." In its first year, First Data had 110 employees and $2 million in revenue, but nine years later it employed 2,000 and produced $50 million in revenue. Today the company has a payroll of 23,000, and a public stock offering in 2015 placed its value at more than $13 billion.

A HIGH-TECH TOWN

Other companies either processing or providing systems for payments are:

- PayPal, which has employed as many as 2,800 at its worldwide operations center in La Vista.
- ACI Worldwide, with more than 500 staffers at 204th and Q Streets, founded in Omaha in 1975 as Applied Communications Inc., but with headquarters now in Naples, Florida.
- TSYS Merchant Solutions downtown, also with about 500 employees.

81. ENERGIZED

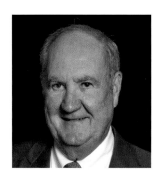

FORBES
RANKS TENASKA
#37
AMONG AMERICA'S
LARGEST PRIVATE
COMPANIES

KEN LAY SAID IN 1986 that he had "no plans now" to move Enron's headquarters from Omaha, but a month later he announced plans to do just that — taking 2,000 good-paying jobs to Houston. The company collapsed 15 years later in financial scandal, and Lay was convicted of fraud and conspiracy.

Enron was a sad chapter for Omaha, and hundreds of local people lost life savings when company stock collapsed.

But one Enron executive declined to leave Omaha when the company pulled up stakes in the

1980s and moved to Houston. Howard Hawks (left) founded his own international independent energy company, called Tenaska, getting its name from "tenacity" and Nebraska.

The company operates and manages power plants nationwide, explores for and produces natural gas and trades commodities. It also owns seven gas-fired plants. Forbes at the end of 2014 reported Tenaska's annual revenue at $9.5 billion.

LOWER UTILITY COSTS

Omaha long has claimed a distinction — and lower costs — because gas, water and electricity are provided not by for-profit companies but by publicly owned utilities. That has contributed to the area's low cost of living. The Omaha Public Power District and the Metropolitan Utilities District are owned by their customers, the citizenry, called "ratepayers."

OPPD'S RESIDENTIAL RATES IN 2014 WERE 14.6% BELOW THE NATIONAL AVERAGE.

MUD'S RATES WERE 19% LOWER THAN THE AVERAGE OF 288 U.S. WATER SYSTEMS.

82. INVENTIONS & INNOVATIONS

NO ONE FROM OMAHA invented, say, the light bulb, the automobile, the Internet or sliced bread. But Omaha is said to be the home of raisin bran, cake mix, butter brickle ice cream, the Reuben sandwich and what many Americans in the 1950s saw as the greatest thing since sliced bread — the TV dinner.

TOP 40 RADIO

Todd Storz of Omaha, scion of the Storz Brewing Co. family, is credited with inventing the Top 40 radio format that became an enduring national standard. The Storz family bought radio station KOWH from the Omaha World-Herald in 1949 and installed Todd as general manager.

In an era of network shows and soap operas, he hit upon a hit format — keep playing the songs that listeners enjoyed, based on jukebox plays and record sales.

By 1951, KOWH was the top-rated independent radio station in the nation, and Storz had launched a radio industry innovation. He also innovated radio promotions, with lucky house address and license plate numbers and even stunts that hid money around town, giving clues on the air about the location. Yes, traffic jams ensued.

Todd Storz, unfortunately, suffered a stroke in 1964 at the height of his career. He died at 39.

TV DINNERS

In 1954, the privately owned Swanson Foods of Omaha introduced what came to be known as the "TV dinner" — the first one containing sliced turkey, cornbread dressing and gravy, peas and sweet potatoes, all packaged in a compart-mentalized aluminum tray. The late Gerry Thomas, a Swanson salesman, never claimed the title some gave him, "father of the TV dinner," but said he did help with the innovation.

The package for the first Swanson TV dinners showed a TV screen with knobs. Each meal sold for about $1 and could be cooked in 25 minutes at 425 degrees. Ten million were sold the first year of national distribution, and Thomas got a $1,000 bonus, a third of his annual salary.

The tray made it to the Smithsonian, and the innovation helped spawn a home fast-food industry. With the later invention of the microwave oven, precooked dinners — no longer called TV dinners — have proliferated by the billions.

THE HARVEY TOILET GASKET

Sometimes one good idea makes all the difference. In 1944, master plumber William Harvey of Omaha invented a pre-formed gasket for sealing toilet bowls, which became the industry standard. From that came the William Harvey Co., which still employs hundreds in Omaha, selling hundreds of arcane items from closet flanges to plastic pipe cements to oils, lubricants and hand cleaners.

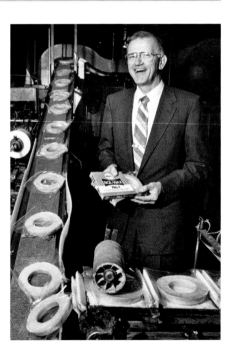

The company has sold millions of the gaskets. Harvey's son, the late Richard Harvey (above), once said: "You cannot start a business on one product. But, fortunately, nobody told my father that."

BUTTER BRICKLE

Butter brickle ice cream was introduced at the old Blackstone Hotel (below) in Omaha in the 1920s.

METAL HAIR CURLERS

Tip Top Products in 1936 patented aluminum hair curlers that sold on a card, four for a dime. After the war, the company expanded, eventually with 24 patents and more than 600 products, including pink foam curlers. Owner Carl W. Renstrom sold out in 1964 to what became the Faberge Co. He died in 1981 and his mansion at 10001 Pacific Street remains, but his adjacent horse farm became home to apartments, office towers and the One Pacific Place shopping center.

CAKE MIX

Chemists for the Omaha Flour Mill, now part of ConAgra, developed and popularized Duncan Hines cake mixes after World War II, though a Pittsburgh company called P. Duff patented an earlier version of gingerbread mix.

REUBEN SANDWICH

Some claim the Reuben sandwich originated at a New York deli owned by Arnold Reuben, but Omahans hold to the story that it was invented at the Blackstone Hotel in the Roaring '20s by local grocer Reuben Kulakofsky (right). Many articles through the years in The World-Herald, the New York Times and Cook's Illustrated magazine, as well as Food Network programs, have been devoted to the sandwich's Omaha origins. The grilled Reuben is made of lean corned beef packed tightly under sauerkraut, with melted Swiss cheese and a slather of Russian or Thousand Island dressing between slices of dark rye bread.

Kulakofsky and his pals, who called themselves "the committee," played a regular late-night poker game in the Fern Room at the old Blackstone at 38th and Farnam Streets. The kitchen would send up a variety of foods for a midnight snack, and Reuben came up with the Reuben, which everyone loved. It now is served at restaurants all over town. The Reuben has many imitators, including turkey Reubens and burgers with Reuben-style ingredients. Even meatless Reubens. But Omahans believe that the original corned-beef Reuben started with an inimitable local guy named Reuben.

RAISIN BRAN

Raisin bran cereal was created in Omaha in 1926 by the Skinner Macaroni Co.

JOHN WIEBE, E. JOHN BRANDEIS AND OMAHA'S SHOPPING HABITS

In Omaha's post-WWII years, the center of shopping wasn't shopping centers but rather was downtown. One day, though, John Wiebe's wife, Harriet, complained in frustration that she couldn't find a parking place. So Wiebe went up in his airplane, flew over downtown and saw the traffic jams. That led him in 1955 to open what was described as the nation's first

enclosed shopping mall, the Center shopping center at 42nd and Center Streets.

The definition of a shopping mall, Wiebe said, later was changed to require two department stores, and he had only one, Younkers. He had invited E. John Brandeis (above), owner of the iconic 10-story downtown Brandeis store, to open at the Center, but Brandeis "wadded up my blueprint and threw it on the floor."

Shopping habits were about to change, and downtown department stores all eventually would depart and move west to shopping centers with plenty of free parking. Wiebe's business battle with E. John Brandeis was an epic Omaha story, but Wiebe said they ended up friends — and Wiebe served as an honorary pallbearer at Brandeis' funeral. They are long gone, but two guys named John and E. John had a huge impact on the shopping history of Omaha.

Brandeis opened the Crossroads at 72nd and Dodge Streets in 1960.

GAME ON: THE BATTLE OF THE MALLS

Wiebe countered in their chess match by opening the Westroads at 102nd and West Dodge in 1968. He bought land and hoped to build Eastroads in Council Bluffs, but it never happened.

WHEN IT OPENED, WESTROADS WAS **5 TIMES BIGGER** THAN CROSSROADS

IN MOTION

A city on the move can't slow down. Fast commutes keep us on the go, parks and playgrounds keep us moving around, schools and universities keep us moving up and our airport and military base keep us free to move about the skies.

83. *EPPLEY AIRFIELD*

A SIGN OF OMAHA'S modesty? Our airport, which handles more than 4 million passengers a year and 70 to 75 departures a day, goes by the plain and simple name Eppley Airfield. But some places with far fewer planes call their airports "international." Eppley has no regularly scheduled commercial flights directly to other countries. Des Moines International, with more than 2 million passengers per year, also has no international commercial flights. Said Don Smithey, who served 20 years as chief administrator at Eppley and then came out of retirement to take over for four years at Des Moines: "You can call it anything you want, but what's important is that you have to provide service."

Eppley, governed by the five-member board of the Omaha Airport Authority, is named for the late Omaha hotelier Eugene C. Eppley, whose donations and interest in aviation helped improve the airport. It conveniently sits four miles north of downtown, about an eight-minute cab ride including a quick jaunt through Iowa.

To get from the airport to downtown Omaha, vehicles take Abbott Drive — which briefly cuts through the town of Carter Lake, Iowa. Very briefly, about 32 seconds.

TAKING FLIGHT

A 60-foot-high bronze artwork by John Raimondi stands at the airport entrance. The sculpture, Dance of the Cranes, was inspired by the graceful mating dance of the sandhill cranes, whose flyway brings them to central Nebraska each spring by the hundreds of thousands. In a ritual that goes back thousands of years, they fly "internationally" from Mexico to Canada, stopping along the Platte River to refuel for the rest of the trip. They feed in cornfields, which, as the birds take flight en masse, become spectacular airfields.

EPPLEY AIRFIELD HANDLED ALMOST **4.12 MILLION** PASSENGERS **IN 2014**

Bob Boozer, who died in 2012, grew up in Omaha and lived here most of his life. He was an All-America basketball player at Kansas State, an Olympic gold medalist and an NBA champion before a corporate career and service on the Nebraska Parole Board. When officials dedicated Bob Boozer Drive, which angles along the railroad tracks from about 162nd and Pacific Streets south to West Center Road near 156th, Bob said people wrongly assumed it was to hail his accomplishments. The real reason, he said with a laugh, was that he had long pestered public officials with the need to pave the road there, near his home. They eventually did so, and put his name on it.

SADDLE CREEK ROAD:
said to be so named because a saddle fell off a wagon crossing a creek there.

JOHN GALT BOULEVARD:
for a character in Ayn Rand's "Atlas Shrugged" who never arrives. The street near 108th and Q Streets, it was felt at the time of development, didn't go anywhere.

MINNE LUSA BOULEVARD:
named for the Florence Pumping Station; from an Indian term meaning "clear water."

EDWARD "BABE" GOMEZ AVENUE:
for a South Omaha resident and posthumous Medal of Honor recipient who died in the Korean War when he fell on a grenade to save fellow Marines.

84. EASY STREETS

OMAHANS DON'T OFTEN have to stew in gridlocked traffic — and they enjoy one of the quickest urban commute times in the country. "Omaha workers have a minuscule commute time (on average) of 15.5 minutes," a California-based real estate blog said in 2014.

It's not as though we've never endured frustrating traffic jams. To alleviate backups on the main arterial of Dodge Street and West Dodge Road, the City of Omaha and the federal government spent a combined $100 million to build the elevated West Dodge Expressway. Drivers immediately said the expressway saved them as much as 20 minutes a day, which surely lowers the length of the average Omaha commute.

THE ELEVATED
WEST DODGE
EXPRESSWAY
OPENED IN
2006

Omaha's transportation grid system eases getting around with a handy and consistent street-naming pattern. North-south streets are mainly numbers. Dodge Street is the main east-west divider, and number streets are known by their relation to Dodge — for example, North 72nd Street or South 120th Street. Simple.

Omaha planners long ago decided to make it easy for people to navigate east-west streets, too. So the policy is that a street keeps it name even if it is interrupted by, say, a half-mile of parkland or some other development. For example, if the street is parallel to Dodge and is nine blocks to the north, it always is Cuming Street.

A 2015 STUDY, BASED ON CENSUS BUREAU STATISTICS, CREDITED OMAHA WITH THE LOWEST AVERAGE ONE-WAY COMMUTE AMONG U.S. CITIES OF MORE THAN 400,000 POPULATION.

RELIGIOUS CONSIDERATION

In the 1950s, the Catholic Archdiocese bought land northwest of 84th and Pacific Streets as the site for Christ the King Church. The street that would run in front of the church was Mason. At the time, tensions existed between Catholics and Masons. Mason Street, though, had nothing to do with the Masonic Order. The street was named after a 19th century judge.

"People joked that it would be funny for Catholics to go to Mass on Mason Street," founding pastor Monsignor Robert Hupp explained years later, "but it was a joke."

In spite of that, the developer of a nearby housing subdivision, a non-Catholic, wanted the street name to be comfortable for Catholics who might buy houses nearby. So he went to City Hall and won approval for a different name for Mason Street between 84th and 90th — Shamrock Road.

85. *PARKS & FITNESS*

PEOPLE FROM ELSEWHERE might not think of Omaha as a top place for parks, recreation and an active lifestyle, but various outside studies indicate that we know how to keep moving and enjoy life.

Omaha received the nation's No. 1 ranking in 2014 from WalletHub, which looked at the 100 most-populated cities, for "how well they accommodate or encourage an active lifestyle." In 2015, WalletHub ranked Omaha No. 2 among the 100 largest metro areas for recreation — based on 27 metrics such as the number of music venues, tennis courts, golf courses, playgrounds and bike-rental facilities, and the quality of walkable parkland. The Trust for Public Land, meanwhile, rated the city's park system 19th-best in 2015, based on access, proximity, size and services. And Men's Fitness magazine ranked Omaha the 23rd-fittest city based on air quality, bike- and walk-friendliness, active lifestyle, access to healthy food and the quality of parks and "urban forests."

Not bad for a town that sometimes endures temperature extremes and isn't necessarily known for its outdoors. Lots of folks belong to health clubs, though, and companies have emphasized personal health for years, spurred on by William Kizer Sr. of Omaha, who founded the Wellness Councils of America in 1987. But an active, fit lifestyle starts with a city's parks and the opportunities for recreation.

PARKS FOLLOW GROWTH

Omahans today enjoy many parks of old and new vintage. Hanscom, Spring Lake, Elmwood, Benson, Fontenelle and Miller were among the early big ones. Lots of neighborhood parks followed, and recent decades have seen the addition of parks around lakes created by flood-control dams, notably Zorinsky (below), Cunningham and Standing Bear. The Fontenelle Forest Nature Center in Bellevue and the Chalco Hills and Walnut Creek recreation areas in Sarpy County are popular, too, as is Mahoney State Park on the Platte River southwest of the metro area.

MEMORIAL PARK

Of all the nice parks, the iconic Omaha green space might be Memorial Park, which first was a private golf course and for a time was envisioned as a housing subdivision. But the owner of a downtown tea shop in the 1940s wrote a letter to The World-Herald suggesting that a beautiful hilltop north of Dodge Street, the city's main east-west arterial, would be the perfect spot for a World War II memorial. The newspaper got behind the idea and so did the community. A curved white memorial containing the names of local war dead was built on the hilltop. Since then, memorials have been added for those in other wars. Memorial Park, across the street from Elmwood Park and the University of Nebraska at Omaha, includes a beautifully tended rose garden. The long slopes attract sledders each winter, and the memorial itself is the site for stirring ceremonies on Memorial Day and Veterans Day. But the park's signature event each summer is the Bank of the West concert and fireworks show before July Fourth.

A 1976 ADDITION HONORS THOSE WHO SERVED IN **KOREA** AND **VIETNAM**

STANDING BEAR

The 685-acre Standing Bear Lake Park, which opened in northwest Omaha in 1977, is a popular site for fishing and boating, picnics and walking on trails. A striking feature is a wind organ by artist Douglas Hollis — vertical metal pipes with holes that produce sound when the wind blows.

It is named for Ponca Chief Standing Bear, whose trial in Omaha led to a landmark 1879 decision that Indians are people under the meaning of U.S. law. It's a dramatic story in which the chief, arrested for returning to Nebraska after he and his tribe had been banished to Indian land in Oklahoma, rose and addressed a federal courtroom, extending his hand.

"That hand is not the color of yours, but if I pierce it, I shall feel pain," he said in the Ponca language, translated in court. "If you pierce your hand, you also feel pain. The blood that will flow from mine will be the same color as yours. I am a man. God made both of us."

U.S. District Judge Elmer Dundy ruled later that the Poncas had been illegally held and ordered their release. Standing Bear returned to his home in Niobrara, Nebraska, and died there in 1908 at about 79.

THE WORLD WAR II MEMORIAL WAS DEDICATED BY **PRESIDENT HARRY TRUMAN IN 1948.**

HANSCOM PARK IS THE **OLDEST PARK** IN OMAHA, BUILT ON LAND DONATED IN **1872**

OFFUTT AIR FORCE BASE and Omaha have enjoyed a good, long-standing marriage. The base and nearby defense contractors employ more than 10,000 military and civilian personnel, and a new $1.2 billion headquarters ensures the base's continuing presence. In addition, many Air Force retirees choose to stay in the area. The result is an annual economic impact estimated at $1.35 billion. "Clearly," said David Brown, president and CEO of the Greater Omaha Chamber of Commerce, "it's just like having another Fortune 500 company."

Omahans are proud that the main landing area on D-Day was code-named Omaha Beach, but the metro area has many other ties to the military, one of which became obvious on another key day in history — 9/11.

Although at least one network news anchor expressed surprise at a report that Air Force One was headed to Nebraska, locals knew in 2001 that Offutt Air Force Base was the perfect place for the president to go in a national emergency. President George W. Bush descended to the famed underground command post that had served the old Strategic Air Command, and then flew to Washington, D.C., to address the nation.

86. OFFUTT AIR FORCE BASE

THE FIRST PHOTOS OF RUSSIAN MISSILE INSTALLATIONS IN CUBA WERE ANALYZED AT OFFUTT

SAC, the motto of which was "Peace is our profession," had helped keep the peace throughout its years at Offutt, 1948 to 1992. Thousands of SAC veterans performed dangerous recon work overseas during the Cold War, and the "Looking Glass" airborne command post, mirroring the one underground, flew round-the-clock flights over the central U.S. for decades. After the breakup of the Soviet Union, the command stood down in a stirring ceremony on a rainy night at Offutt, with Gen. Colin Powell, chairman of the Joint Chiefs of Staff, declaring: "Well done, SAC."

A museum dedicated to the Strategic Air Command and the nation's other air and space achievements, including a "Looking Glass" and numerous other planes, sits southwest of Omaha near the Platte River on Interstate 80.

PRESIDENT KENNEDY VISITED OFFUTT AND SAC TO EXPRESS GRATITUDE AFTER THE CUBAN MISSILE CRISIS IN 1962.

A CRISIS AVERTED, IN PART BY AN OMAHA NATIVE

A hero of the 1962 Cuban missile crisis was an Omaha native, SAC pilot William B. Ecker. His low-level reconnaissance flight — at 350 to 400 feet — produced photos proving the existence of Soviet ballistic missiles in San Cristobal, Cuba. Flak from below narrowly missed his plane. After the crisis ended and the threat of nuclear war subsided, President John F. Kennedy pinned a Distinguished Flying Cross on Ecker, a 1942 graduate of the old Omaha Tech High School. His photo hangs in the Smithsonian's National Air and Space Museum.

OFFUTT HISTORY

Offutt, home to the U.S. Strategic Command and to the 55th Wing, traces its beginnings to Fort Crook in the 1890s. The air base, sitting next to the city of Bellevue just south of Omaha, is named for Lt. Jarvis Offutt (above) of Omaha, who died while flying in France during World War I. In 1940, the Army Air Corps picked Offutt as the site of the Glenn L. Martin bomber plant (right), which produced 1,585 B-25 Marauders and 531 B-29 Superfortresses. Two B-29s — the Enola Gay and Bockscar — were modified there to carry the atomic bombs that fell on Hiroshima and Nagasaki, ending World War II.

THE WAR ROOM

In the event of nuclear attack, the Strategic Air Command would have directed its forces from an underground war room at Offutt. A new electronic system was installed in 1963, replacing an earlier system that relied on hand-marked designations on maps and charts.

AIR FORCE GEN. CURTIS LEMAY GREETED HARRY TRUMAN AT OFFUTT IN 1952 FOR A PRESIDENTIAL INSPECTION OF SAC.

THE BUFFETT CENTER

(NAMED FOR INVESTOR WARREN BUFFETT'S LATE COUSIN AND HIS WIFE) IS DESIGNED FOR PERSONALIZED, GENE-BASED TREATMENT, AND WILL ADD MORE THAN 100 PHYSICIANS OVER THE NEXT FEW YEARS.

A 2015 STUDY ESTIMATED UNMC'S ANNUAL ECONOMIC IMPACT ON NEBRASKA'S ECONOMY AT $2.4 BILLION

WIDELY KNOWN IN THE national medical community for its cancer and transplant centers, as well as for its treatment of Ebola patients, the University of Nebraska Medical Center in Omaha is more than a center of education, research and patient care. It's also an economic engine that a civic leader and philanthropist said is in "the business of healing."

If UNMC and its hospital partner, the Nebraska Medical Center, were a private business, said Walter Scott, it would be Omaha's fifth Fortune 500 company. Since 2007, UNMC facilities represent an investment of $700 million.

Dr. Harold Maurer (at top), UNMC's former chancellor who later served as its chief fundraiser, knows how to wedge his way into the wallets of the wealthy. Quipped Scott: "As cancer patients, the most alarming thing, maybe the most terrifying words that can be said to us, are 'You have cancer.' As philanthropists, the words that scare us are 'Dr. Maurer has a new idea.'"

At an event celebrating the groundbreaking for the $323 million Fred & Pamela Buffett Cancer Center, Scott said: "Omaha is home to this new and exciting business — the business of healing. And the value of that, my friends, is priceless." Scott, chairman emeritus of Peter Kiewit Sons' Inc., was a donor for the cancer center, Omaha's largest public-private project.

"To make something like this happen, it was really the right time, the right place, the right people and the right community."

Dr. Ken Cowan, director of the Fred & Pamela Buffett Cancer Center

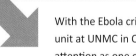

THE UNMC EBOLA TEAM

With the Ebola crisis of 2014, the biocontainment unit at UNMC in Omaha became a focus of national attention as one of the few places in the United States to treat the disease, which started in Africa. Concerned that Ebola could spread, national TV commentator Rachel Maddow asked: "How do we replicate Omaha?"

The World-Herald named the Ebola team — led by the unit's medical director, Dr. Phil Smith, and associate medical director Dr. Angela Hewlett (above in center) — plus nurses, lab workers, respiratory therapists, care techs and two dozen physicians, as the "Midlanders of the Year." Dr. James Linder, former interim president of the University of Nebraska, said the honor spoke to UNMC's foresight in creating the biocontainment unit a decade earlier. "The fact that Dr. Smith and his team were ready and trained for this crisis — so well-trained, in fact, that their treatment guidelines are now being studied by other health organizations across the United States — is a testament to the vision of the University of Nebraska and UNMC."

IMPACT OF UNMC AND CREIGHTON

Among its peers in similarly populated areas, the academic medical industry in Omaha had the largest economic impact on the communities it serves. That is according to a 2012 analysis by the Association of American Medical Colleges, based on the combined impact of the University of Nebraska Medical Center and the Creighton University Medical Center.

As a city, the Omaha market outranked medical industry centers in peer markets such as Rochester and Albany, New York; Little Rock, Arkansas; Tucson, Arizona; and Albuquerque, New Mexico, all with similar metro populations. Paul Umbach, president of Tripp Umbach, the consulting firm that conducted the analysis, said Omaha is poised to take yet another step. "Omaha is already a major economic player in the academic medicine industry," Umbach said, "with an exceptionally bright future to join the top-tier centers."

FOR SEVERAL YEARS, U.S. NEWS & WORLD REPORT HAS RANKED CREIGHTON NO. 1 IN THE MIDWEST FOR ACADEMIC QUALITY AND NET COST OF ATTENDANCE.

The university's first college to be named for a person honors Charles Heider, an investment banker and 1949 Creighton grad who died in 2015. Two years earlier, he had donated the largest gift in Creighton's history, the amount undisclosed but surpassing the previous record of $50 million.

A HIGH-TECH BEGINNING

Creighton University is named for a 19th century high-tech pioneer who strung telegraph wires across the West. Edward Creighton, born in Ohio to immigrant parents, had moved to Omaha in the city's infancy. His telegraph crews met up with a company's workers stringing wire eastward from San Francisco, beating them by a week to the meeting point in Salt Lake City in 1861. "This being the first message over the new line since its completion to Salt Lake," he wired his wife in Omaha, "allow me to greet you. In a few days, two oceans will be united."

The wealthiest Nebraskan of his time through his Western Union holdings, Creighton became a founder of the First National Bank of Omaha. It is said he inspired the hastened construction of Union Pacific rails across the West. When the golden spike was hammered in Utah in 1869, completing the transcontinental railroad, the electrifying moment was relayed to the world over Creighton's telegraph lines.

After his death at 54, his widow, Mary Lucretia Creighton, donated money to start the university, founded in 1878. John Creighton, his brother and business associate, contributed much money and time to the university, which considers him a co-founder.

88. CREIGHTON UNIVERSITY

CREIGHTON'S FUTURE

Creighton isn't finished. It celebrated two groundbreakings in 2015: a new Creighton University Medical Center, costing $135 million, on the campus of Bergan Mercy Medical Center; and a $35 million medical building at 24th and Cuming, adjacent to the longtime CU campus.

One of the nation's best college soccer stadiums, a state-of-the-art indoor athletic center and a new home for the college of business are among recent additions, fueled in part by a $350 million fundraising campaign.

CREIGHTON UNIVERSITY IS SUCH an Omaha institution that it's easy to take it for granted. But it is unique. Among the 28 Jesuit universities in the United States, Creighton is the only one that includes not only an undergraduate curriculum but also law, medical, dental and allied health schools and, as part of CHI Health, a hospital. Omaha is crawling with Creighton-educated doctors, lawyers, nurses, dentists, physical and occupational therapists, teachers, businesspeople and others. The university's footprint on its hometown is huge.

And just as Omaha has grown, Creighton has expanded its reach. The city's recent improvements along the riverfront, including a convention center-arena, a baseball stadium and a performing arts center, have been met more than halfway by CU, growing eastward toward the river.

Creighton educates more than 8,000 students per year — 4,000-plus undergraduates and a similar number of postgraduates. They come from all 50 states, and about two-thirds of the students come from outside Nebraska.

Creighton's national profile was raised in 2013 by its move to the Big East Conference. Bluejay teams now compete with universities in metropolitan New York, Philadelphia, Chicago, Washington, D.C., Milwaukee, Indianapolis and Cincinnati. The exposure, it is hoped, will help with student academic recruitment. Omaha fans support the men's basketball team, with average attendance of about 17,000, ranked fifth in the country.

THE SCHOOL COUNTS MORE THAN 60,000 ALUMNI IN 89 COUNTRIES

89. *UNIVERSITY OF NEBRASKA AT OMAHA*

ALUM AT THE TOP

John Christensen, UNO chancellor since 2006, is the first person with a degree from the school to serve in its top post. The grandson of Danish immigrants and the son of a drywall contractor, Christensen graduated from Omaha Benson High and the old Dana College in Blair, Nebraska. Like a number of UNO students, he was the first in his family to attend college.

He earned a master's degree in speech-language pathology from UNO and a doctorate from the University of Kansas. In 1989, he was a visiting professor in Beijing and visited Tiananmen Square as protests mounted, but was told by a dean to leave the country immediately — which Christensen did just before government massacres began.

A former dean of UNO's College of Education, he has visited metropolitan universities across the country and says UNO is one of the most beautiful. Unlike most, which are landlocked, UNO has increased its land mass by expanding to the south.

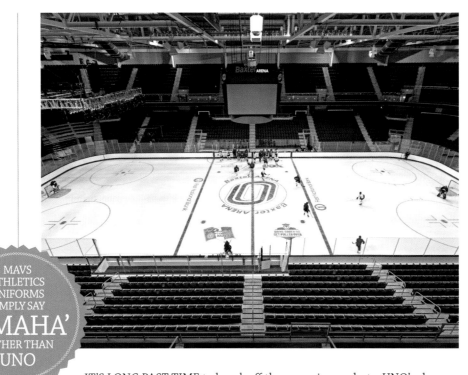

MAVS ATHLETICS UNIFORMS SIMPLY SAY 'OMAHA' RATHER THAN UNO

IT'S LONG PAST TIME to knock off the pervasive modesty, UNO's chancellor says, and to tell the school's story in a no-brag-just-fact way. Fact is, the University of Nebraska at Omaha has raised its profile and its reach in many ways, with campus academic expansion, a move to NCAA Division I in sports and the 2015 opening of 7,898-seat Baxter Arena.

Founded in 1908, the school became the municipal Omaha University in 1930 and entered the state system in 1968 as the University of Nebraska at Omaha. UNO was a commuter-only school until the late 1990s, when the first campus housing opened. The university since has expanded to the south on the former site of the Aksarben racetrack, which is home to more student housing, the Peter Kiewit Institute for engineering and technology and Mammel Hall, home of the business college.

Roskens Hall was renovated as the new home of the College of Education, and the former Engineering Building became the College of Public Affairs and Community Service. The university also opened a new Biomechanics Research Building and a Community Engagement Center. And in 2011, the Carnegie Foundation for the Advancement of Teaching reclassified UNO from a master's degree-granting to a doctoral/research institution.

UNO continues to educate locals, with 87 percent of the student body coming from Nebraska, the highest percentage in the NU system and the most ethnically and racially diverse. More students than ever enjoy global experiences, with expanded study abroad through the university's International Studies and Programs. Meanwhile, more than 2,000 international students from 117 countries study at UNO.

The alumni association achieved a milestone of 100,000 living graduates, of whom 43,000 live in the Omaha area. "I can't imagine a more exciting time at UNO than what we're going through right now," alumni president and CEO Lee Denker said in 2013. "Enrollment is up, and when you look around campus you see cranes for new buildings. We're doing things that our alums from 50 years ago could not imagine."

BAXTER ARENA

UNO opened its $82 million, 7,898-seat Baxter Arena (at left) in 2015, home to the university's signature hockey team. Adding to the excitement was that the Mavericks earlier in the year made it for the first time to the "Frozen Four," the final four of NCAA Division I hockey.

UNO basketball and volleyball teams also play at the arena, which is available for other community events, such as high school graduations and the Aksarben Coronation & Scholarship Ball. Naming rights were purchased for $4 million over 10 years by Baxter Auto, whose late leader, Tal Anderson, was a UNO alum and athlete.

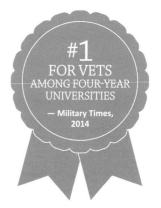

#1 FOR VETS AMONG FOUR-YEAR UNIVERSITIES — Military Times, 2014

"There are moments in the history of institutions that are monumental, and this is one of those very special times in the life of UNO."

— **John Christensen, chancellor, on the 2015 opening of Baxter Arena**

ETC.

Let's finish our look at what's cool about Omaha with a potpourri of thoughts and images. From our not-flat landscape to our food, our traditions, our politics and even to songs about Omaha (some quite funny), there's a lot to say — and always more to tell.

STAR CHEF

Omaha native and celebrated chef Clayton Chapman (left) worked in the dish pit at Mother's Good Food in north Omaha at 15 and later at M's Pub in the Old Market before attending culinary school in Chicago and experiencing French cuisine in Europe. Back in Omaha, he headed the V. Mertz kitchen at 21, and at 24 opened The Grey Plume, a "seasonally driven, eco-minded, locally sourced" restaurant that was named one of America's greenest.

Chapman twice has been nominated for a national James Beard Award for "rising star, chef of the year" and twice for "best chef, Midwest region." Cooking Light magazine earlier named him one of the nation's seven "trailblazing chefs."

#2 FOODIE CITY — Livability.com, 2015

90. FOODIE CITY

OMAHA LONG HAS been known nationally for steaks, but a number of sources rank the city highly for much more than a great filet or ribeye. Omaha now stakes its reputation as simply a great Foodie City. The Wall Street Journal noted "Omaha is a mecca for steaks, of course, but the immigrant neighborhoods in South Omaha have excellent ethnic restaurants." In addition, Money magazine in 2015 named Omaha one of America's top five places to live, based largely on the food scene. The magazine lauded the farm-to-table movement of several restaurants that get their produce and meat from local farms, and editors liked it that diners can get the great food at "Omaha prices."

FOX NEWS SALUTED OMAHA AS A "HIPSTER CHIC" CITY WHOSE FOOD EXCEEDED ITS REPUTATION, WITH SPECIAL MENTION OF MICROBREWERIES.

#3 UNLIKELY FOODIE CITY — Fox News

BIG MAMA'S KITCHEN

Omaha's best-known soul food restaurant, Big Mama's Kitchen, has bared its soulfulness on national TV, with appearances on the Food Network. Viewers met Patricia "Big Mama" Barron (above) and her daughter, Gladys, who manages her mother's two restaurants — the original Big Mama's Kitchen and Big Mama's Sandwich Shop. Episodes in 2013 showed the family's funny behind-the-scenes life and repartee, concluding with a traditional weekly family meal at Big Mama's house, where the down-home menu began. Big Mama also appeared on host Guy Fieri's "Diners, Drive-ins and Dives."

ETHNIC FOOD

Omahans and visitors enjoy a great variety of food choices, and not just at the annual three-day Taste of Omaha at the riverfront Heartland of America Park and nearby Lewis & Clark Landing.

Motor-coach tours annually arrive in Omaha with visitors to enjoy such programs as "Ten Countries Without a Passport." Buses might stop at the Lithuanian Bakery for torte samples or at St. John's Greek Orthodox Church for spanakopita. The Nebraska Scottish Society has offered tea-tasting at the Joslyn Castle, and French restaurants might serve up steak frites a la Parisienne.

At the Bohemian Cafe on 13th Street south of downtown, visitors see how aromatic kolaches are made and hear the longtime jingle, "Dumplings and kraut today … at the Bohemian Cafe."

91. SEXY & FERTILE

A HEADLINE IN USA Today, no lie: "Sexy Omaha?" Seriously, why the question mark? As if there's a question at all. In any case, the article quoted actress Anna Kendrick, who was in George Clooney's "Up in the Air," filmed partly in Omaha. "I swear to God, Conor Oberst (nationally known singer) came out of there, and where we were staying was near all these record shops and used T-shirt shops. It was like every person walking down the street was going to be the next big thing."

Further reason to eliminate the question mark: Fit Pregnancy magazine ranked Omaha the seventh-best city in the nation for having a baby. The mag used 50 criteria, including low maternal mortality, breast-feeding rates, access to day care, stroller friendliness — and fertility. "Omaha is this really great Midwestern city," said the magazine's Peg Moline in an interview with NBC News. "Very affordable, great air quality." Another reason for the high rating, she said, is that "my researchers tell me it is high sperm quality, too." "Oh, good," said NBC's Natalie Morales. Peg: "Really important." Natalie: "Good to know." Peg: "It's a very fertile city."

7TH
BEST CITY FOR
HAVING A BABY
— Fit Pregnancy magazine

"I thought Omaha was pretty sexy."

— Actress Anna Kendrick, on being in Omaha to shoot "Up in the Air"

92. AKSARBEN

NEWCOMERS TO OMAHA soon come across a name that strikes them as odd, and it's certainly unusual — Aksarben. Originally hyphenated as Ak-Sar-Ben, the name has left a permanent imprint on Omaha in various ways, including entertainment, volunteerism and philanthropy. During the economic downturn of the 1890s, a group of Omaha businessmen thought they could put some dazzle into their city after returning home from a Mardi Gras trip to New Orleans. So the Knights of Aksarben adopted the story of the mythical kingdom of Quivira and began honoring leading families at a glittery coronation ball at which a play-acting "archbishop" crowned a costumed king and queen, whose names were closely guarded secrets. The ceremony continues to this day.

The fall-harvest October event, with princesses and escorts promenading to the music of an orchestra, holds to the practice of selecting a 60-ish king, usually a leader of business or education, and a 20-ish queen, the daughter of parents active in civic affairs. The organization explains that the mature king embodies achievement, and that the youthful queen symbolizes the community's hope for the future. The coronation ball pays tribute to other accomplished citizens in a "court of honor," and it raises money for scholarships and other good causes. Though the coronation ball is seen as a high-society event, Aksarben through the years has catered to everyday folks. For decades, it sold memberships at modest prices, and the "member shows" brought some of the biggest names in entertainment to the Aksarben Coliseum for weeklong gigs — Frank Sinatra, Bob Newhart, George Burns, Sammy Davis Jr., Bob Hope, Tony Bennett and many others.

TOM OSBORNE WAS AKSARBEN KING IN 2007

Q: WHAT DOES AKSARBEN MEAN?

A: IT'S NEBRASKA SPELLED BACKWARD. IT WAS MADE POPULAR BY AN OMAHA BUSINESSMAN WHO SAID, "EVERYTHING SEEMS TO BE GOING BACKWARDS."

THE AKSARBEN CORONATION HAS BEEN AN OMAHA TRADITION SINCE THE 1890s

Miss Peggy Doorly
Her Majesty
The Queen + Ak-Sar-Ben
XXXIX

For most of the period from 1920 to 1995, Aksarben was widely known as a big-time racetrack. From the start of May into August, the place produced the sounds of the Sport of Kings — the bugler's call to the post, the ringing of the bell and the announcer's "And they're off!" Hear the hoofbeats around the far turn, the crowd noise rising as the horses and jockeys headed down the stretch. The track known as Ak also was an economic engine. On weekends, busloads of fans from Kansas City, Des Moines and elsewhere filled Omaha's motels and restaurants. The "backside" was almost a town of its own, with a track kitchen, stables and early-morning workouts. For a few big stakes races on Saturdays that drew such top jockeys as Eddie Arcaro and Willie Shoemaker, crowds reached 30,000. Marion Van Berg and son Jack Van Berg saddled many winners and became national hall of fame horse trainers. In 1985, Aksarben enjoyed a record year for attendance and pari-mutuel betting. Then it suddenly went downhill. Greyhound racing and casinos in Council Bluffs, as well as lotteries and keno parlors, cut deeply into attendance and betting at Ak. A decade after the record year, the race course closed. The track, the grandstand and the coliseum eventually were demolished.

FOR A FEW BIG STAKES RACES, ATTENDANCE AT THE RACETRACK REACHED **30,000**

OTHER NAMESAKES

Businesses for many years have adopted the name Aksarben — or Ak-Sar-Ben: chimney sweeping, electrical contractors, guttering, heating & air conditioning, plumbing, roofing, siding, carpet cleaning, drain cleaning, hairstylists and more. The track also gave the Aksarben name to its old neighborhood south of Elmwood Park.

93. POLITICS

POLITICALLY, OMAHA IS DIFFERENT from the rest of Nebraska, a reliably GOP "red state." Omaha has plenty of reliable Republicans but also lots of die-hard Democrats — party registrations are more evenly split in Omaha, and Democrats over the years have held a number of city and county elected offices.

Omaha elective offices are officially nonpartisan, though candidates' party affiliations are known. Mayors have come from both parties, and Omaha's redevelopment of the past two decades has occurred under both. For example, Republican Hal Daub pushed for the bond issue that financed most of the riverfront convention center and arena (now called the CenturyLink Center) and Democrat Mike Fahey pushed for construction of the downtown stadium for the College World Series (TD Ameritrade Park).

Since Omaha's Home Rule Charter took effect in 1957, the municipal government has operated under a mayor-council — sometimes called "strong mayor" — form of government because the mayor is chief executive. Some other cities' day-to-day operations are run by city managers.

After 12 years with Democrats in the top city office, a Republican was elected to a four-year term in 2013 — Jean Stothert. She is a former intensive-care nurse and member of the Millard school board and Omaha City Council.

JEAN STOTHERT IS THE FIRST WOMAN ELECTED MAYOR IN OMAHA'S HISTORY

ERNIE CHAMBERS

Ernie Chambers of Omaha hasn't mellowed. The longest-serving state senator in the history of Nebraska continues to argue, rant, cajole, incite, provoke, outwit and at times persuade. He can charm, too, though that's not the Ernie most people see. In debate, he can go for the jugular. Out in the middle of the country, far from the seas, he continually makes waves.

Born in 1937 — by coincidence, the year that Nebraska instituted its unique one-house Legislature — he grew up in north Omaha feeling the sting of racism. He earned a law degree from Creighton University but never took the bar exam. Instead of practicing law, he has helped make laws. For years he cut hair at the Spencer Street Barber Shop, but lists his occupation as "defender of the downtrodden." First elected to the Legislature in 1970, he served nearly four decades until Nebraskans imposed term limits — to get rid of him, he says. In 2012, he again was elected.

A POLITICAL INDEPENDENT

Chambers, who refers to partisans as Repelicans and Demagogues, has used his skill with legislative rules to block bills or force compromise. The liberal publication Mother Jones described him as "left of San Francisco" and credited him, among other things, with legislation that abolished corporal punishment in schools, gave women equal status in the state pension system and created district elections in some local governments.

OFTEN THE ONLY AFRICAN-AMERICAN IN THE 49-MEMBER LEGISLATURE, HE SAID A FEW YEARS AGO ON NATIONAL PUBLIC RADIO:

"IF ALI BABA CAN HANDLE 40 THIEVES, CERTAINLY I SHOULD BE ABLE TO HANDLE 48 WHITE PEOPLE IN THE LEGISLATURE."

A CAPITAL IDEA

In jest, some who have ingested too much political bickering in the nation's capital have suggested a move to a great place — Omaha. A Washington Post article a few years ago lamented: "Let's send the federal government to Omaha. Let's move all the agencies and restrictions and Jersey barriers and chain-link fences out of Washington. Just think of the enormous economic boom for Omaha when all the lawyers and lobbyists settle there." Not long after that, a law professor at the University of California-Berkeley suggested moving the U.S. Supreme Court to Omaha — lock, stock and gavel. His article in a publication of the University of Minnesota Law School, where he previously taught, was headlined: "Moving the Supremes to the Heartland: The Case for Omaha." The court seemed to be increasingly political, he wrote, adding that when justices attend high-powered cocktail parties and diplomatic receptions, it makes the court even more political. "It would be nice for the justices to think of themselves as more like the lawyers, judges and other honest folks of Nebraska, and less like the movers and shakers in Washington."

ONLY IN MAINE AND NEBRASKA

IS IT EVEN POSSIBLE TO SPLIT THE ELECTORAL VOTE. ALL OTHERS USE THE WINNER-TAKE-ALL SYSTEM.

IOWA CAUCUS

In presidential election years, Iowa and its caucuses count. Nebraska and its spring primary, for the most part, do not. But Omahans don't necessarily feel left out. Council Bluffs gets frequent visits from the presidential hopefuls, who also run ads on Omaha TV stations.

UNIQUE ELECTORAL VOTE

Omaha holds a distinction in American politics — the only place to deliver a presidential electoral vote different from the rest of its state. The Nebraska Legislature voted in 1991 to allocate electoral votes by district.

It happened in 2008, when the Omaha-dominated 2nd Congressional District voted for Barack Obama. The Obama campaign had targeted the Nebraska 2nd District, foreseeing the mathematical possibility that the Electoral College outcome could turn on one vote — with a 270-268 tally rather than 269-269. While it was clear that Republican John McCain would win at least two districts in GOP-dominated Nebraska, Obama campaign manager David Plouffe later wrote, "We thought we could steal the 2nd District, around Omaha, where our organization was strong and we already had ads on the air to reach Iowa voters."

Obama won the 2nd District by 3,000 votes – but didn't need it, amassing 365 electoral votes to win the presidency. In 2012, he lost Nebraska's 2nd District. But the experience showed that in Nebraska, Omaha could be a "swing city."

1988 OMAHA VP DEBATE

A memorable footnote in American political history occurred at the Omaha Civic Auditorium in 1988 at the vice presidential debate between Democrat Lloyd Bentsen of Texas and Republican Dan Quayle of Indiana, both U.S. senators. After Quayle said his experience in Congress was comparable to that of John F. Kennedy before he ran for president, Bentsen delivered the line that he had practiced:

"Senator, I served with Jack Kennedy. I knew Jack Kennedy. Jack Kennedy was a friend of mine. Senator, you're no Jack Kennedy."

In the years since, "You're no (fill in the blank)" has become part of the political lexicon. But Quayle and running mate George H.W. Bush won the election over Michael Dukakis and Bentsen.

94. 'THE BROOM MAN'

MAYBE, JUST MAYBE, God sent the Broom Man to Omaha to help us see better. Remembered in city lore for his six decades of walking streets and neighborhoods selling brooms door to door, the Rev. Livingston Wills maintained a blind faith in people. Literally. The ordained minister, blind from birth, was a fixture and an icon, almost universally recognized in his black suit and black hat, broomsticks over his shoulders.

Inspiring Omaha with his perseverance and kindness, he might walk 10 miles a day. "He walked 10 feet above the average man," a fellow minister said at the Broom Man's 2008 funeral. "He was a great man, leaving a great legacy upon Omaha."

A bishop compared him to the itinerant prophet Elisha. A Catholic priest called Wills, longtime piano-playing pastor of Tabernacle Church of Christ Holiness, "the saint of Omaha."

Pastor Wills always said he trusted in the Lord to use him and watch over him. Friends affectionately joked that whistling was his sonar, helping him avoid bumping into things. Reverend Wills walked with the Lord until his death at 91. Mourners, some of whom held brooms at his gravesite, were urged to think of him whenever they heard the hymn, "Sweep the Devil Out."

He never carried a chip on his shoulder, just brooms — and a lifelong message of good will.

"Whenever I got sore about my eye, I thought of the Broom Man. He never gave up."

— Bicycle shop owner Jay Farlee of Omaha, describing his own struggle with failing eyesight

WILLS ONCE ESTIMATED THAT HE CALLED ON
100 HOMES A DAY,
COVERING A DISTANCE OF EIGHT TO 10 MILES.

---

95. UNIQUE POSTAGE STAMP

"It was really exciting, except that I couldn't say anything. How many people get that kind of opportunity? My one attempt at immortality!"

— Robin Welch, the Omaha ballerina depicted on the 1978 U.S. postage stamp

WHEN THE U.S. Postal Service in 2011 changed its longtime rule that you had to be dead to be depicted on stamps, it came to light that the image of a widely known Omahan was used years earlier — the lively Robin Welch. She was the young ballerina pictured in 1978 when a postage stamp cost barely a lick, 13 cents. "She was told not to tell anyone," her daughter revealed, "because she would technically have to be dead."

Ah, technicalities. Welch had been living in New Haven, Connecticut, when a photographer from Yale University asked her to pose for the stamp. The secret was kept for decades after her image became part of a tribute to "USA Dance." Welch (at left teaching in Omaha) became a professional in New York City at 17 and toured the U.S. and Europe before becoming artistic director of the Omaha Theater Ballet. She now operates Robin Welch Dance Arts, having long ago put her stamp on the art of ballet.

96. POETIC

OMAHA OF THE EARLY 21st century bears little resemblance to the smoky, early-20th century city that "works to get the world a breakfast," as Pulitzer Prize-winning poet Carl Sandburg wrote in 1922. Now a sleek and modern city heavy on the service industry — rather than on heavy industry itself — Omaha is more white collar than blue and isn't the roughneck that Sandburg observed. It recently was named the No. 1 city for tech workers, and its diverse and strong economy allowed it to maintain the lowest unemployment rate among the 100 largest U.S. metro areas during the recent Great Recession.

CARL SANDBURG

Pulitzer Prize-winning poet
(1878-1967)

Even in the 1950s, though, with the South Omaha Stockyards, Omaha remained the nation's largest livestock market. But Swift, Armour, Cudahy and Wilson, the "Big Four" meatpacking plants — the term for slaughterhouses — closed their plants in the 1970s as the industry became decentralized.

Omaha still benefits from its place in the middle of America's breadbasket. Sandburg's "Omaha" contains images that today look prescient.

He wrote of "green grass circles around Omaha" long before Valmont Industries became a world leader in center-pivot irrigation. And in reading that "a span of steel ties up the kin of Iowa and Nebraska across the yellow, big-hoofed Missouri River," it's easy to picture the Bob Kerrey Pedestrian Bridge that links Omaha and Council Bluffs.

Sandburg lived in Galesburg, Illinois, like Omaha surrounded by cornfields, and he wrote a group of poems under the heading "Cornhuskers," which wasn't specifically about Nebraska. His most famous poem, though, was about Chicago: "Hog butcher of the world . . . Stormy, husky, brawling, City of Big Shoulders."

Omaha's shoulders still may not be as big as Chicago's, but the Big O can do the heavy lifting and pull its own weight — even if it no longer works so hard to get the world a breakfast.

OMAHA'S OLD MARKET OF LONG AGO

Long ago, Sandburg is said to have stayed at the Mercer Hotel in today's lively Old Market, the historical fruit and vegetable market downtown. The hotel was at the northwest corner of 12th and Howard Streets. (Wheatfield's restaurant is at the ground level today.) From that block, it's believed, he wrote "Sunset From Omaha Hotel Window."

"SUNSET FROM OMAHA HOTEL WINDOW"

Into the blue river hills
The red sun runners go
And the long sand changes
And to-day is a goner
And to-day is not worth haggling over.
Here in Omaha
The gloaming is bitter
As in Chicago
Or Kenosha.
The long sand changes.
To-day is a goner.
Time knocks in another brass nail.
Another yellow plunger shoots the dark.
Constellations
Wheeling over Omaha
As in Chicago
Or Kenosha.
The long sand is gone
and all the talk is stars.
They circle in a dome over Nebraska.

"OMAHA"

Red barns and red heifers spot the green
grass circles around Omaha — the farmers
haul tanks of cream and wagon-loads of cheese.

Shale hogbacks across the river at Council
Bluffs — and shanties hang by an eyelash to
the hill slants back around Omaha.

A span of steel ties up the kin of Iowa and
Nebraska across the yellow, big-hoofed Missouri River.

Omaha, the roughneck, feeds armies,
Eats and swears from a dirty face.
Omaha works to get the world a breakfast.

SANDBURG
WASHED DISHES
AT THE MERCER HOTEL BUT SAID HE DIDN'T GET PAID

97. FLAT WRONG

TODAY, ONE OF THE many misconceptions by people elsewhere is that Omaha is flat. No, it's a river city, and so it's naturally hilly. A visiting East Coast urban planner, Jonathan Barnett of Philadelphia, acknowledged a few years ago that his mental picture had been flat-wrong. "When I first came to Omaha," he said, "I was struck by how hilly it is." A geography professor, meanwhile, said in The World-Herald that Omaha is hillier than Des Moines, Kansas City, Minneapolis or Milwaukee. But isn't Omaha on the Great Plains? A number of businesses, after all, long have used "Great Plains" as part of their names. And some maps include Omaha as part of the Plains. But some geographers say that the tree-laden topography of Omaha and eastern Nebraska is "riverine" and that the Plains actually start to the west of the city. Drivers traveling westward on I-80 near a hilltop rest stop suddenly come upon a wide vista where the Plains begin — the Platte River Valley.

"ISN'T OMAHA FLAT?"

NO, IT'S NOT. AND NEBRASKA IS ONLY THE 20TH FLATTEST STATE.

STEAM ENGINES AND DUMP CARS RAN ON SPECIAL TRACKS TO LOWER **DODGE STREET**

98. *SING IT OUT*

OVER THE YEARS, sometimes seriously and often comically, "Omaha" has appeared in quite a number of songs — including a long-form commercial that pokes fun at the city's famous friendliness.

The satirist Stan Freberg, in a bit for Omaha-based Butter-Nut Coffee, had a cast member enthusing: *"What have they got in Omaha? They've got happier people. Whistlin' people. Happy because they live in Omaha!"* That seven-minute spoof from 1958 also lampooned the era's big musicals. Songs included "Omaha Moon" and "I Look in Your Face and I See Omaha."

Some might dream of a true anthem for Omaha, perhaps waiting to be written. But it's good to know that so many songwriters and singers have honored the city, even if some wiseacres just focus on the "ha" of Omaha.

HOMETOWN ACT

311 has opened concerts with "Omaha Stylee," a salute to its hometown, "where shows are more fun."

MOBY GRAPE'S
"OMAHA" **#95**
WAS LISTED AS
IN ROLLING STONE'S "100 GREATEST GUITAR SONGS OF ALL TIME"

ESPN often plays the Counting Crows song "Omaha" during the College World Series: *"Omaha, somewhere in middle America. Get right to the heart of matters. It's the heart that matters more."*

The Los Angeles rock band Rilo Kiley, before signing with the Omaha-based Saddle Creek Records, sang: *"Then we'll go to Omaha, to work and exploit the booming music scene."*

Charlie Daniels sang: *"I think I'm gonna re-route my trip, I wonder if anybody'd think I'd flipped, If I went to L.A., via Omaha."*

Bob Seger told of *"a long and lonesome highway east of Omaha."*

The Everly Brothers sang: *"Everything's there, my love and my laughter. It's all in Omaha."*

Grand Funk Railroad immortalized the *"four young chiquitas in Omaha, waitin' for the band to return from the show. Feelin' good, feelin' right, it's Saturday night. The hotel detective, he was outta sight."*

Bob Dylan sang that, *"I'm gonna ride into Omaha on a horse."*

Groucho Marx long ago sang the nonsense song, *"There's a place called Omaha, Nebraska, in the foothills of Tennessee."*

Waylon Jennings sang: *"Omaha, you've been weighin' heavy on my mind. Guess I never really left at all."*

For traditionalists, there's "The Omaha Song," which proudly proclaims, *"Omaha, Omaha, greatest place you ever saw. Come along, join the throng, 'cause you simply can't go wrong – I'll say it's great in Omaha, Omaha."*

ORIGINAL HYMN

One of Christendom's most beloved and inspiring hymns, "On Eagle's Wings," was first played in Omaha. Long since translated into dozens of languages and played in the presence of popes, presidents and prime ministers, the soaring and poetic composition was written not for the famous but for the funeral of a retired Omaha accountant and World War II veteran. In 2014, a plaque to commemorate its first playing was installed at St. Robert Bellarmine Catholic Church.

The hymn was composed by seminarian Michael Joncas for the funeral of H. Douglas Hall, father of Joncas' friend and fellow seminarian, Doug Hall. In April 1976, Joncas put the handwritten, finishing touches on the composition at the Halls' family home. That evening, he played his guitar and sang at the John A. Gentleman mortuary and did so again at the next day's funeral at St. Robert. (The family still owns the original musical chart, written in pencil.)

It was recorded in 1979 and soon was played often during Pope John Paul II's visit that year to the United States. After that, said Father Hall, "It just exploded across the whole Christian scene in America." The hymn has comforted millions at funeral Masses as well as in the aftermath of mass tragedies, such as the 1995 Oklahoma City bombing and at services for firefighters and other victims of 9/11 terror.

"And he will raise you up on eagle's wings,
Bear you on the breath of dawn,
Make you to shine like the sun,
And hold you in the palm of his hand."

— "On Eagle's Wings"

MICHAEL JONCAS

A priest of the Archdiocese of St. Paul and Minneapolis, Joncas has written more than 300 compositions. He was 24 when he composed the piece based on Psalm 91 and Isaiah 40:31, the latter of which says those who hope in the Lord will soar on wings like eagles.

Omaha •

OKLAHOMA

OMAHA & OKLAHOMA ARE NOT THE SAME PLACE!

99. CONFUSION

OMAHANS SOMETIMES HEAR IT — people from elsewhere confusing Omaha and Oklahoma. The letters in "Omaha" do appear in "Oklahoma," but Omaha is a city and Oklahoma is a state, and they're 400 miles apart. Sure, "the wind comes sweeping down the plains" toward Omaha, too, but that lyric belongs to "Oklahoma!"

After witnessing a fender-bender in Kentucky, one Omahan provided his contact information and said he was from Omaha, which brought a follow-up, "What city in Omaha?" Flights to Omaha have been announced as going to Oklahoma. When an Omahan working in Washington, D.C., mentions where he is from, he often hears something like, "Oh, I have a cousin in Tulsa." An Omaha business-man who traveled throughout the U.S. and Europe said he "was constantly introduced as being from Oklahoma."

To some folks on the coasts, Omaha and Oklahoma are vaguely out there somewhere in the middle of the country, so maybe the confusion is natural. People in the Sooner State are called "Okies," but Omahans aren't known as "O-mies." At Omaha's 150th-birthday celebration at Heartland of America Park, just before the fireworks, the Omaha Symphony segued from "There Is No Place Like Nebraska" into an upbeat — you guessed it — "Oklahoma!" O boy. Nothing against the fine state of Oklahoma, but let's hope everyone — sooner or later — will know the distinction between Oklahoma and Omaha.

THE LATE POPE JOHN PAUL II ONCE TOLD AN OMAHA ARCHBISHOP THAT THE INDIAN NAMES FROM PLACES IN THE MIDDLE OF AMERICA CAUSED HIM CONFUSION.

100. SISTER CITIES

OMAHA ENJOYS SISTERLY relationships with six cities around the world, and 2015 marked the 50th anniversary of the Omaha Sister Cities Association. The whole notion grew out of the embers of World War II. Gen. Dwight D. Eisenhower became president of the United States and proposed "citizen-to-citizen diplomacy" as a way to preserve peace. Sister cities promote understanding through personal visits and programs focused on "arts and culture, youth and education, economic and sustainable development and humanitarian assistance." Omaha's longest relationships are with cities in Japan and Germany, the countries we fought in war.

OUR SISTER CITIES:

- Shizuoka, Japan (1965)
- Braunschweig, Germany (1992)
- Siauliai, Lithuania (1996)
- Naas, Ireland (2002)
- Xalapa, Mexico (2005)
- Yantai, China (2011)

A 40TH-ANNIVERSARY GIFT FROM SHIZUOKA

In 2005, Omaha sister city Shizuoka, Japan, donated a replica of its Sunpu Castle gate, which was placed in Omaha's Lauritzen Gardens. Shizuoka Mayor Zenkichi Kojima and then-Mayor Mike Fahey took part in the dedication. The gate is set in front of a 30-foot hill meant to evoke Mount Fuji, near Shizuoka.

AN IRONY OF HISTORY

On the night of June 19-20, 1945, American B-29s dropped incendiary bombs on a coastal city in Japan named Shizuoka. The name of one of the planes: City of Omaha. Shizuoka was home to a Mitsubishi aircraft engine factory. Besides an estimated 2,000 deaths on the ground, two B-29s collided, killing 23 U.S. airmen. Monuments to the Japanese dead and to the American airmen stand near each other on a Shizuoka hilltop. In 2015, Omahans and Shizuokans celebrated 50 years of friendship, with many events and with delegations from each city visiting the other. In September, the Shizuoka Philharmonic played with the Omaha Symphony at the Holland Performing Arts Center. And Japanese-born sculptor Jun Kaneko of Omaha created an 8-foot-tall ceramic Tanuki, popular as a "raccoon dog" in Japanese folk culture, as a gift to Shizuoka.

DAVID BROWN

The Association of Chamber of Commerce Executives presented its top individual honor, the Chairman's Award, to Omaha Chamber President and CEO David Brown. He also was humorously roasted as an Omaha Press Club "face on the barroom floor." A friend teased him about the chamber's slogan, "We Don't Coast," claiming that another slogan Omaha had considered was "Landlocked and Lovin' It!"

THE GREATER OMAHA CHAMBER OF COMMERCE WAS NAMED THE **TOP CHAMBER IN THE U.S. IN 2015**

THE CREATIVE TEAM

Omaha writers, producers and artists collaborated on "We Don't Coast." Steve Gordon (below), part of the team, explained the slogan: "It's a very much stand-up-and-pound-your-chest moment — I'm from the Midwest, any questions?"

101. *WE DON'T COAST*

DESPITE ALL THE national socioeconomic and livability rankings, and all the improvements to our civic landscape, it's in our Omaha nature that we don't boast. There's also no reason for complacency. Hence: We Don't Coast.

That's the image-boosting slogan the Greater Omaha Chamber of Commerce selected for a $6 million campaign to better recruit businesses, jobs and talent to the six-county area. It's a branding that its creators call "loaded with attitude."

Omaha copping an attitude? Cool. A little bit of swagger and confidence to replace the old self-deprecating diffidence could make a nice difference. "You think you know us," a narrator says drily in a chamber video, about to explain that you don't.

Our pioneering spirit "led us away from the coasts." In Omaha, we don't wait for things to happen, we make them happen. We live active, authentic, inspired lives in the middle of America, offering a rugged backbone and the "strong, broad shoulders on which this country sits." We are "constantly moving, climbing upward."

That's the goal. In the Omaha area, the chamber says, we don't coast. We innovate, we unite, we launch, we inspire. We kick, punch and create. We don't coast. We make waves. We boogie. We accomplish more together. We can't slow down now, and we sure ain't gonna coast.

ACKNOWLEDGMENTS

MOSTLY FOR THE BETTER, Omaha has changed a lot — but not in the way that some local and national civic leaders imagined more than a half-century ago. Some of their predictions call to mind the old prime-time "Jetsons" TV cartoon show of the early 1960s, with airborne personal vehicles.

Writing in the mid-20th century, one Omaha executive predicted that by the early 21st century, "Trips to the moon and the planets will be as commonplace then as airplane travel within the United States is now." An advertising executive wrote: "Guided-missile passenger flights will be carrying passengers from New York to Los Angeles in 30 minutes. Escalator sidewalks will be everywhere." Another business leader predicted that a typical Omahan would work only three or four days a week, five hours a day, and "would fly his own rocket ship on a weekend trip to Mexico City or Rio or the Riviera."

Those predictions were off by more than a little bit, so I surely won't try to predict what Omaha will look like at midcentury and beyond. Suffice it to say I have been pleased to live in Omaha and watch it grow and to write about today's Omaha in this book. But I sure didn't do it alone.

My thanks start with World-Herald book editor Dan Sullivan and designer Christine Zueck-Watkins, who produce books for the newspaper. Their organizational and graphic skills far exceed mine. They kept the project moving forward and offered great advice. Executive Editor Mike Reilly not only gave me time away from column-writing, but also provided guidance and encouragement.

The text of this book is largely the product of having covered Omaha for 45-plus years at The World-Herald. At one time or another, I have written about practically every topic in these pages. So in preparing the book, I mined my columns through the years for pithy, fun facts about our city; but I also owe gratitude to all of my talented colleagues whose coverage of Omaha proved to be a great resource. At times along the way, colleagues Henry Cordes, Kevin Coffey, Alissa Skelton, Bob Fischbach, Robynn Tysver and Nancy Gaarder kindly answered my requests for specific expertise. Many thanks to discerning copy editors and to photo imaging specialist Jolene McHugh, who helped bring hundreds of pictures to these pages. The newspaper's chief librarian, Jeanne Hauser, was always quick to respond with research help.

Mike Kelly in 1970

For me, writing about Omaha inside a hard cover has been a nice culmination to a career that isn't over yet, but started with colleague Steve Jordon introducing me to officers on the police beat when I was 21. The author of "The Oracle and Omaha," about Warren Buffett's connections with his hometown, Steve continues to write for the paper in peak-of-career form and has been the greatest friend through good times and bad. For paying me to line up words for a living, a great gig, I thank former World-Herald publishers Harold W. Andersen and John Gottschalk, and our current boss, Terry Kroeger. Woody Howe, Jack Holley, Bob Dorr and the late Bob Pearman are among those who had great influence on me in my developing years. Today I look around the newsroom and marvel at all the talent and hard work of reporters, editors, photographers and others.

I thank my wife, Barb, for her constant support, as well as our grown children Laura, Kevin, Bridget and Nick, all of whom married wonderful spouses and have produced nine grandkids for us at this writing. I thank World-Herald readers for being so interested in our community. And for being so wonderfully supportive when Bridget got hurt really bad, but miraculously survived and then thrived.

This is a good place, Omaha. Who knows what the future holds?

Those earlier predictions were sealed in a time capsule at the 1958 opening of the Guarantee Mutual Life Co. headquarters in Omaha, to be reopened on the company's 100th anniversary in 2001. Alas, in life there are no guarantees — Guarantee Mutual didn't make it to 2001 under that name. It was sold in 1999, and the capsule was quietly opened the next year.

The predictions came during the Cold War, and the Strategic Air Command based in the Omaha area helped keep peace and avoid a hot war. Some had written that it would be a miracle if World War III were avoided. Former President Herbert Hoover darkly wrote for the Omaha time capsule that he could only ask questions about the early 21st century, including, "What would be left after nuclear war?"

We're still here. Medical advances, too, have lengthened lives. Former Mayor Johnny Rosenblatt, who suffered from Parkinson's disease, predicted that 21st century science "will have conquered today's fatal illnesses." Scientists in Omaha are working on that.

No, we're not flying in personalized rocket ships. But you don't have to be a rocket scientist to understand that Omaha has propelled itself forward in recent decades and laid a foundation for future generations. Problems surely remain. As difficult as it is to predict the future, though, the local forecast is hopeful. May Omaha enjoy mostly sunny days, with just enough rain to precipitate good growth for all.

Mike Kelly

UNIQUELY OMAHA
BY MICHAEL KELLY

ABOUT THE AUTHOR

In a 45-year World-Herald career, Michael Kelly has covered police, courts and city hall, spent a decade as sports editor and sports columnist and written a column in the general-news sections for nearly a quarter-century. He was the lead writer of the 2010 World-Herald book "Big Red Rivals" as the Nebraska Cornhuskers bade farewell to universities that had served as football opponents for many years.

In recent years, Mike twice has won first place for column-writing in the eight-state Great Plains Journalism Awards and received the first-place national award for commentary and column-writing in 2003 from the American Society of Newspaper Editors. He is a frequent speaker in the Omaha area and has performed in and emceed many Omaha Press Club Shows.

EDITOR
Dan Sullivan

DESIGNER
Christine Zueck-Watkins

PHOTO IMAGING
Jolene McHugh

CONTRIBUTING EDITORS
Bob Glissmann
Rich Mills
Pam Richter
Kathy Sullivan
Pam Thomas

INTELLECTUAL PROPERTY MANAGER
Michelle Gullett

DIRECTOR OF MARKETING
Rich Warren

DIRECTOR OF PHOTOGRAPHY
Jeff Bundy

PRINT AND PRODUCTION COORDINATOR
Pat "Murphy" Benoit

EXECUTIVE EDITOR
Mike Reilly

PRESIDENT AND PUBLISHER
Terry Kroeger

REPRINT INFORMATION
Omaha World-Herald photos are available from the OWHstore. Call 402-444-1014 to place an order or go to OWHstore.com.

PHOTOGRAPHERS INDEX